The New Scapegoats:
Colored-On-Black Racism

The New Scapegoats: Colored-On-Black Racism

Kwame Okoampa-Ahoofe, Jr.

iUniverse, Inc.

New York Lincoln Shanghai

The New Scapegoats: Colored-On-Black Racism

iUniverse books may be ordered through booksellers or by contacting:

iUniverse
2021 Pine Lake Road, Suite 100
Lincoln, NE 68512
www.iuniverse.com
1-800-Authors (1-800-288-4677)

LCCN: 2005924118

ISBN-13: 978-0-595-35011-7 (pbk)
ISBN-13: 978-0-595-79716-5 (ebk)
ISBN-10: 0-595-35011-9 (pbk)
ISBN-10: 0-595-79716-4 (ebk)

Printed in the United States of America

For Abena B. and Nana Yaa A. Amoh; Abena A. Okoampa-Ahoofe; Leah Afua Gyamfuaa; Samuel Odoi-Sykes II, and the yet-to-be-born scions of our clan; that my passionate struggle for sociopolitical, cultural, economic and racial justice shall make their own, much, much easier.

Contents

ACKNOWLEDGMENTS

I wish to acknowledge the following people:

Karl Botchway, Vincent B. Thompson, Steve Panford, Seth Asumah, Ibipo Johnston-Anumonwo, John Marah, Roger Gocking, Abu S. and Nana Q. Abarry, Walter and Miatta Hai Smith, Edna Sarr, William K. Egyir, Don Thomas, Eddy Wong, Bernadine Brown, Roberta Kramer, Marian Parish, Ralph Nazareth, Joseph Dowling, Chris Schwertman, Randy Hayman, Guy Pollio, Harold Bellinger, John Ostling, Louis Rivers, Sean Fanelli, Kwasi and Serena Ohene, Kwaku Oduro, Evans Kwaku Owusu and Daniel Adofo Kwasi Kissi Nyamah, Dmitri Urnov, Norman Spencer and Charles Owusu.

INTRODUCTION

An article appeared in the ***New York Amsterdam News*** of February 3-9, 2005, titled "Tensions Between Africans and African Americans Surface Again." Actually, as has been characteristic of this Black, historic newspaper of record, the preposition "between" was pluralized into "betweens," for whatever such linguistic solecism may be worth. Years ago, when I doubled as some sort of nondescript literary critic and editor for the ***Amsterdam News***, I was asked by the editor-publisher to submit a list of what I considered to be the One-Hundred Classical Books authored by global Africans; I shortly learned, to my utter chagrin, that the editor-publisher's more inclusive way of describing African-Americans, including other African-descended people outside continental Africa, was to expansively but vacuously label them as Black People. Africans patently appeared to belong to another world and another civilization altogether. And so, I ended up with a list that was almost totally devoid of continental African presence. But what was more significant was the fact that having determined that I was not supposed to be able to spell words correctly, the editor-publisher, then just out of New York University's journalism school, promptly changed my spelling of "Millennial" to "Millenial." I protested to no avail; for the editor-publisher's father owned the newspaper and, besides, had it not always been a commonplace fact that editors know best and know it all?

Written by Jennifer Cunningham, the aforementioned article reported of raging fisticuffs between largely Francophone African street vendors in Harlem and some hostile African-American residents of that historic quarter of New York City. Mr. Ya-Ya, a 32-year-old sales associate at Harlem Kids, a departmental store, whose African nationality was not given by the freelance reporter for the ***Amsterdam News***, claimed to have been assaulted by some unspecified number of African-Americans whom Mr. Ya-Ya claimed to have prevented from shoplifting. The assault must have been quite severe, for the alleged victim claimed to have called for police intervention. In the end, he only sustained what the victim termed as a broken nose. However, what appears to have hurt and pained him even more was that during the course of his assault, Mr. Ya-Ya also claimed that his assailants had taunted him by shouting: "You Black monkey, go back to Africa."

It may also be of some significance, as adumbrated above, that the bulk of the continental Africans who have been involved in such violent incidents have almost invariably been Francophone and have tended to possess the barest minimum of Western-type education. Consequently, one is hardly surprised to learn that the problems that these continental Africans have with their African-American kin border largely on what might aptly be designated as cultural misunderstanding and economic competition. And as Mr. Bill Fletcher, of the venerable, Afrocentric lobbying group TransAfrica, rightly noted, these two familial groups, or kin, harbor pernicious misconceptions about one another. On the one hand, continental Africans, being often for the first time exposed to the fabulous economic wealth of the United States, and almost totally ignorant about much of Black history, observe the apparent existence of great opportunities and simply presume that the relative African-American socioeconomic and political marginality is squarely due to the abject indolence of the hitherto proscribed African-American. Matters are further complicated by the fact that the remarkable numbers of well-educated Africans who enter the United States, particularly Anglophone Africans, often end up securing respectable middle-class job, largely out of the reach of many an urban poor African-American citizen of the United States. These naïve, recent-immigrant critics often woefully fail to take account of the at once blistering and daunting psychological climate which many an African-American has had to endure for some two to four centuries of forced residence in the so-called European New World.

On the other hand, many under-educated and mis-educated African-Americans often tend to glibly ignore the intricate dynamics of history, by summarily envisaging almost every continental African whom they encounter, both here in the United States and abroad, as the veritable scions of callous and myopic African collaborators in the infamous Trans-Atlantic Slave Trade. And here also, matters are not in the least ameliorated by the likes of Professors Henry Louis Gates, Jr., and Lani Guinier, otherwise highly schooled African-Americans and elite educators, who do not seem to have mastered the effective utilization of a good education in the proactive cause of global African liberation and development. In his textual and filmic documentary titled **Wonders of the African World**, for instance, Professor Gates, a distinguished brain behind Harvard University's African-American Studies project, unreservedly incriminates continental Africans for the Trans-Atlantic enslavement of African-Americans. And as we have observed elsewhere, the Gatesian damage, jointly sponsored by the British Broadcasting Corporation (BBC-TV) and America's Public Broadcasting System (PBS-TV) at a reportedly whopping tune or sum of $10 million, will take at least the better part of a generation to remedy or countervail. And it is largely this lethal blight on the otherwise salutary landscape of global African scholarship that has necessitated the initiation and development of this series of articles. On this score, therefore, **The New Scapegoats** is more of a communal and global African response, or rejoinder, for that matter, to the deleterious ideology of Gatesianism, that a personal attack, as some readers have come to regard our series which ran in the **New York Beacon** weekly from July 2004 to February 2005.

Affectionately,
Kwame Okoampa-Ahoofe, Jr.
Bronx, New York
March 1, 2005.

1

On the nineteenth anniversary of my immigration, here, into the United States, I find myself having to vehemently defend my ethnic identity and nationality against some prominent—and almost distinguished, if I weren't a little afraid to so affirm—African-American cynics who would have the fairly successful likes of me entirely banished from the elite hallways of the august American academy, as it were. The sole, or overriding, rationale of these self-serving and self-appointed champions of the diasporic African cause is that the likes of me have preponderantly and unjustifiably benefited from Affirmative Action programs at the damnable expense of *full-blooded*, whatever that means, African-Americans. Interestingly and regrettably, the thrust of the argument of these cynics threatens to confirm what many a right-wing or racist white-American—as well as their Black conservative collaborators—has maintained since the foundation of the modern American republic, the myth of African-American inferiority. Fortunately and hearteningly, recent advanced studies in genetics and the social sciences have put paid to such ideological balderdash. And so for some African-American alumni of Harvard University to be grouping and vigorously strategizing about ways and means of either drastically reducing the remarkable presence of recent African and Afro-Caribbean immigrant students at these Ivy League institutions, or entirely banishing them, reeks of the phantasmagorically interesting and ludicrous (see "Top Colleges Take More Blacks, But Which Ones?" **New York Times** 6/24/04).

Interestingly, the preceding article was also published on the very day that this writer legally contracted a conjugal relationship with his fellow very recent African immigrant wife, with the noble intention of establishing a family and becoming an integral part of the greater diasporic African community. But, perhaps, my most excruciating pain emanates from the fact that I decided, against my late father's advice and better judgment, it now appears, to earn a doctoral degree in African-American Studies at Temple University; and now I feel like an abject fool for this venture (or is it an adventure?)

For those of you who have been reading my articles, in various African and African-American newspapers, for the past seventeen (17) years may pretty much appreciate it, when I observe that I have spent almost every moment of these years championing the global African cause, our collective cause, that it. And so I quite well know a little bit of what I am talking about when I firmly assert that this rather weak-minded and bizarre attempt at driving a wedge, both culturally and ideologically, between African-Americans and continental Africans, as well as our Afro-Caribbean kinfolk, would not wash; rather, it is apt to galvanize our inviolable resolve to logically draw global African people and their history full circle, as it were, by uniting us more than ever before.

According to Professors Henry Louis Gates, Jr. and Lani Guinier, both of Harvard University, the new definition of **African-American** is "one all of whose grandparents were born in the United States, descendants of slaves." Needless to say, in our kind of cosmopolitan African world, one would be hard put to identify any African-American family that has not conjugally or genetically intermingled with a continental African or Afro-Caribbean individual or family. And it is precisely this historical fact which makes the Gatesian-Guinierian argument unpardonably reek of the sophomoric and preposterous. And here, also, the definition of **African-American** becomes quite protean and outright murky, since such palpable ideological praxis as racism appears to be of tangential or secondary significance in the minds of these critics. For both Professors Gates and Guinier are bona fide products of biracialism, the former via conjugal affinity, and the latter by parentage. What is more, in the case of Professor Guinier, whose mother is white, we are also apprised of the fact that her father immigrated from Jamaica. In brief, therefore, going by her own logic, Ms. Guinier who is only half American, and then only half-Black, ought not to have been admitted to Harvard University where, we learn from other sources, her father once served in quite a prominent academic and administrative capacity. Maybe somebody ought to have reminded Professor Guinier of the adage which perspicuously observes that: "Those who live in glass houses should not throw stones." Then again, maybe it is her guilty conscience that has prodded her to assume such awkward and supercilious posture—otherwise known as **grandstanding**. And here, I honestly confess that I don't know much about Ms. Guinier, except for that passing moment when her enthusiastic bid for a political appointment, during the heady Clinton administration, was summarily quashed, on ideological grounds, by the Republican-dominated United States Congress. Then, rather than take her admittedly capricious defeat in stride, like the rest of her ilk, Ms. Guinier brusquely decided to take it personally by ignobly impugning the credibility of the Clintons, almost as if the latter were to blame for her effusive ranting on the so-called **Critical Race Theory**. Like Professor Gates, much of what Ms. Guinier has published is barely readable. They simply do not communicate effectively; and on the few occasions that they do communicate, what either of them has to say does not carry much heft in both logic and meaning.

Unlike Asante who sought to instill the requisite confidence and cultural self-worth and appreciation in our youth, for instance, Professor Gates once wrote an opinion piece for ***Newsweek*** magazine (or was it ***Time***?), making a mockery of Professor Karenga and the latter's proactive founding and successful institutionalization of the august Kwanzaa Festival. Back then, if memory serves this writer accurately, Professor Gates sneered to the damnable effect that Los Angeles, California (where Mr. Karenga resides) was no Lagos, Nigeria. But what amuses this writer is Professor Gates' brazen linguistic vulgarity in asserting that "We [African-Americans] need to learn what the immigrants' kids have so [that] we can bottle it and sell it." Needless to say, it is precisely this ***Feeding-Bottle Mentality***, the inordinate craving for the facile, or easy-way-out, on the part of some African-American educators and intellectuals that is squarely to blame for the raging bleak landscape of the proverbial African-American academy.

2

In their most recent diatribe against the relatively high undergraduate admission of continental Africans and African-Caribbean students at Harvard University, as well as other Ivy League institutions, Professors Henry Louis Gates, Jr. and Lani Guinier observed that "in the high-stakes world of admissions to the most selective colleges—and with it, entry into the country's inner circles of power, wealth and influence—African-American students whose families have been in America for generations were being left behind" (Rimer and Arenson, **New York Times** 6/ 24/04). The obvious assumption, and implication, was that the so-called indigenous African-Americans were being left behind solely because continental African and African-Caribbean students were being unjustifiably favored. Interestingly, as Rimer and Arenson's article, titled "Top Colleges Take More Blacks, But Which Ones?" attests, even in the age of Affirmative Action, academic aptitude or merit is very much de rigueuer; in other words, the policy of Affirmative Action is more of a sociopolitical corrective, rather than a racially essentialistic gimmick.

In sum, the policy of Affirmative Action was enacted to ensure that African-Americans, as well as other ethnic and racial minorities, who have been historically proscribed and marginalized would be afforded a ***relatively equal opportunity*** to access the bountiful civic and cultural amenities, or facilities, of the American mainstream. And as the likes of this writer have pointed out time and again, Affirmative Action is more of a moral obligation than merely an unsavory enactment of ***Alms*** or charitable assistance to the intellectually undeserving and socio-economically irrelevant. On the contrary, it is in the ineluctable recognition of the seminal and massive contributions of Africans to the development of modern American civilization. And on this score, we emphasize the unique African contributions to the foundation and development of these United States of America. For the perennial enslavement of millions of continental Africans implied the logical, systematic and chronic impoverishment of the primeval continent. And, indeed, it is in view of the preceding that the patently puerile and outright sophomoric attempt by Professors Gates and Guinier to divide the global African community deserves our utmost contempt and condemnation. On this score, one may aptly ask: Would Mr. Gates and Ms. Guinier also question the phenomenal influx of recent European and Asian, as well as Latin-American, immigrants into the most elite academic institutions of the United States? If not, then these two high-end academics could best be described as pathologically self-hating and woefully alienated. Or, maybe they simply find continental Africans and African-Caribbeans to be more vulnerable and therefore easy prey to attack with the barest minimum expectation of condign, or logical, reprisal? If the latter turns out to be the case, then these Ivy-drunk popinjays are grossly mistaken. For we, their preys, intend to fight back in a way that would make Mr. Bush's all-out war on terrorism seem like the proverbial piece-of-cake.

On the other hand, looking at the apocalyptic conditions of the post-King and post-Malcolm era, as well as the desolate conditions of Liberia, Sierra Leone, the Democratic Republic of the Congo and Rwanda, this is the last phenomenon that anyone could unleash on another, particularly a kinsman or kinswoman.

Another problem, or question, that Professors Gates and Guinier fail to address is the glaring historical fact that the overwhelming majority of the most important and influential African-American politicians and leaders did not graduate from Harvard College, Yale or any of the other much-touted Ivy League institutions, as they would have their audience believe. These luminaries, on the contrary, largely attended the best of the Historically Black Colleges and Universities and diligently worked their way into the mainstream of American society. And on this honor roll, we list David Dinkins, Charles Rangel, Thurgood Marshall and Hazel O'Leary. Some of them simply attended some of the best public universities and colleges, among them Maulana (Ron) Karenga and Ronald Brown. Black America has even produced two United States surgeon-generals none of whom attended an Ivy League institution. And here, we are also reminded of the two most prominent diasporic African members of the Bush II cabinet, Gen. Colin L. Powell and Dr. Condoleezza Rice, perhaps also the most brilliant cabinet appointees, Black or white, in recent times. Then there is also the aforementioned sterling case of late Clinton administration secretary of commerce, Mr. Ronald Brown. And so just where do Professors Gates and Guinier come by their logic and statistics regarding the institutional sources or provenance of Black power and leadership? Of course, we are all very much aware of the historical circumstances that created the foregoing state of affairs. However, it is also interesting to observe that during the last three decades, or so, since the enactment and implementation of Affirmative Action programs, one which facilitated the unprecedented influx of African-Americans into mainstream American institutions of higher education, the provenance, or seminal sources, of the production of African-American leadership has not significantly altered. The bulk of mainstream Black leadership continues to be produced by such Historically Black

Colleges and Universities as Howard, Morehouse, Spellman, Hampton, Tuskee-gee, Lincoln, Wilberforce and Fisk. Even the greatest African-American thinker of the twentieth century, Dr. W. E. B. DuBois, was a veritable and vintage prod-uct of Fisk University, a historically Black college. He would later attend Harvard and Berlin Universities, but not until the seminal and indelible contours of his intellectual prowess had been fabricated at Fisk University. And here, the name of African-American creative genius James Weldon Johnson bears mentioning. It is also interesting to recall that decades after he had left Harvard University, as the first African-American scholar, historian and sociologist to have been awarded a doctoral degree in white-America's flagship academy, Dr. DuBois frequently quipped that the salient difference between Harvard and Fisk universities lay almost squarely in the fact that the faculty at Harvard was more famous, but not necessarily any better intellectually and pedagogically than that of Fisk.

It is also quite amusing for Professors Gates and Guinier to assume that just about anybody who opts to attend Harvard, or any other Ivy League establish-ment, for that matter, opts to do so primarily because an Ivy imprimatur, as it were, guarantees one unfettered access or "entry into the country's inner circles of power, wealth and influence." Indeed, while this assertion cannot be totally denied, or discounted, Professors Gates and Guinier may be pleasantly bewil-dered to learn that the kind of Anglophone education experienced by continental Africans from Ghana, Nigeria, Kenya, Uganda, Zambia, Botswana and Tanzania, among others, sets them intellectually and professionally on a course of cultural refinement of the highest caliber. For the kind of intellectual activity that appears to have kindled the spirits of Mr. Gates and Ms. Guinier pretty much inheres the Euro-colonial education of the nationals of the countries listed above. Unfortu-nately here in the United States, at least in recent times, higher education has been woefully vulgarized and morphed into a value-tagged commodity. In other words, the significance or value of one's education in America is reckoned almost absolutely in terms of dollars and cents. This may largely account for why many an African-American youth these days appears to be much more eager to join the vapid and materialistic culture of the rap-music industry. Last year, for example, a former African-American schoolmate of mine abruptly quit his academic posi-tion—as an assistant professor—at one of the City University of New York cam-puses to join the hip-hop (or rap-music) industry, because Dr. John Bullshitsky (not his real name) had aptly determined that the work of an educator is not ade-quately appreciated or respected here in the United States. I don't remember my former colleague complaining to me, or anybody else, for that matter, that his disillusionment with the proverbial academy stemmed from what he perceived to be the inordinate influx of continental Africans and African-Caribbeans into the academy. Professors Gates and Guinier might more productively expend their remarkable intellectual energies and political influences in finding solutions to such indisputably grievous problems as the preceding, rather than thrashing about wildly looking for external causes and scapegoats for the apparent crisis in African-American higher educational prospects.

3

While I am not personally a product of the Ivy League, nevertheless, I feel disconsolately affronted by recent assertions by Harvard Professors Henry Louis Gates, Jr. and Lani Guinier to the effect that the relatively higher intake of continental Africans and African-Caribbean students by "the most selective colleges," the expression of these critics, has a converse correlation with the intake of African-Americans at such Ivy League institutions as Harvard and Yale. This state of affairs, Professors Gates and Guinier maintain, has a deleterious impact on the future of those African-Americans who gloat at the fact that their ancestors were enslaved here in the United States. In their opinion, it is these "descendants of slaves" (their own terminology) towards whom the corrective policy of Affirmative Action was enacted. As I pointed out earlier, even assuming that the preceding argument contains any iota of validity, the problem still remains regarding how to scientifically identify these "descendants of slaves," particularly, since these two privileged Harvard eggheads insist on clearly differentiating recent continental African immigrants, as well as their African-Caribbean counterparts, from what these critics term as "indigenous African-Americans" (See "Top Colleges Take More Blacks, But Which Ones?" **New York Times** 6/24/04). And as we noted earlier, there is almost no single African-American family that has not had any conjugal relationship with any continental African or African-Caribbean since the pre-colonial era of American history. And to be certain, it is outright fatuous for anyone to try to even make such an assertion, since there was no time over the last 500 years during which continental Africans were totally cut off from their diasporic kin in the Americas, or anywhere else, for that matter. It is also rather embarrassing and unfortunate for otherwise quite astute and erudite academics like Professors Gates and Guinier to brazenly scapegoat continental Africans and Black Caribbeans for the perceived intellectual and academic handicap of "their people." Of course, the latter quote comes from these critics themselves.

Indeed, those of us who have studiously followed his academic and professional career during the past two decades were not in the least surprised by Professor Gates' latest diatribe. Several years ago, for instance, the renowned Yale University graduate undertook a filmic project flamboyantly and sensationally titled ***Wonders of the African World***, a three-part series which was widely tele-vised by PBS across the country, and other parts of the world, in which Professor Gates, sporting Harvard University T-shirts, made an incredible mockery of ancient African civilizations. Gloatingly quoting inveterate anti-African racists like Richard Burton, a nineteenth-century British explorer and historian, Mr. Gates described African civilizations as patently unimpressive and one that was largely mythological. And so one can quite understand why he is so visibly upset and shaken by the apparently incontrovertible fact that continental Africans who enter the United States with the primary intent of seeking an education generally excel their African-American counterparts. In fact, the entire point of Mr. Gates' ***Wonders of the African World***, an undertaking estimated to have cost at least $10 million, was to prove that Africans were a bunch of banana-chomping patho-logical savages and barbarous slavocrats who deserved no sympathy from the glo-bal community of humanity, particularly the Western human being. In the end, Mr. Gates appeared to endorse the fact that some of his ancestors, the continental African part, were shipped to the Americas and enslaved.

Looking at the relatively bleak African socioeconomic and political landscape, the sneering and cynical narrator of ***Wonders of the African World*** told the par-able of a group of misguided African-Americans who departed the United States in the early 1960s to permanently settle in Ghana, the erstwhile Gold Coast. Having arrived somewhere in Accra or Cape Coast, Ghana, these Afrocentric fanatics went to the beach one night and, during a ritual exorcism, threw their American passports into the Gulf of Guinea in order to thoroughly obliterate the loathsome demons of their enslaved ancestral past. One week later, the narrator quipped with an imperious air of clairvoyant maturity—what our elders call intellectual prescience or wisdom—these same African-Americans who would have nothing more to do with the United States, their opprobrious past, returned to the beach with torch-lights, frantically looking to recover their rejected pass-ports. We are not told by Professor Gates, the snub-nosed narrator of ***Wonders of the African World***, whether these obviously misguided African-Americans ever recovered their disowned passports, and also what explanations any of these prodigals offered the American consulate as tangible reasons that qualified them to be issued new passports. We can only surmise, as Professor Gates appeared to expect of his audience, that these ***Nine-Day Afrocentrists*** went back to the American consulate in Accra, on all fours, and prayerfully pleaded with the con-sular officer or consul to be immediately lifted out of this hellhole of an ancestral homeland.

It is also significant and interesting to recall that when he was asked by a white PBS-TV executive, shortly after his *Wonders of the African World* had been extensively televised on that prestigious network, as to exactly where he stood in relation to continental Africans, Professor Gates promptly retorted: "The Africans are my distant cousins. Nothing more, nothing less. I am an American born in Piedmont [or is it Keyser?] West Virginia, and I intend to remain as such." The implication here, it goes without saying, was that Africans were some quadrupeds or lower primates who, at best, could be sympathized with, or tangentially pitied, rather than amicably interacted with, or worst of all, even loved. We know quite well that like all ardent racists, Professor Gates, *the racial and cultural hybrid*, would, at this juncture, be prompted to mention the names of such distinguished continental African friends and associates of his like Professors Wole Soyinka and Chinua Achebe, of Nigeria, and Anthony Kwame Appiah, Ghana, to vehemently dispute our assertion. But it would be even more interesting to hear just what these longtime friends and staunch ideological supporters would have to say in response to Professor Gates' dastardly attempt at flushing the remarkable continental African presence out of the august hallways of Harvard University. And here, also, it is significant to observe that Professor Henry Louis Gates, Jr., is largely what he is career-wise because of the beneficent foresight of Nobel Literature Laureate Mr. Wole Soyinka. The narrator of *Wonders of the African World* has himself amply testified to this fact, and so we will not belabor it at this juncture. Suffice it to say, nonetheless, that most of his encounters with continental Africans appear to have been positive; and so it is quite bewildering that Professor Gates would choose to pick on Africans for a patently gratuitous intellectual and cultural fisticuff. And one would that he ought to, by now, know that this is a battle that he simply cannot win; for Professor Gates is not likely to get such far more savvy scholars as Cornel West, or even Julius Wilson, to enlist in his rather myopic and patently fatuous and divisive cause.

4

When Harvard University professor of African-American Studies Henry Louis Gates, Jr., laments the fact that there are relatively more continental African and African-Caribbean undergraduates enrolled in that celebrated flagship academy than "indigenous" African-Americans, he either dishonestly or erroneously presumes the crux of this perceived problem to be one of recent development or mintage. Consequently, the proud West Virginian native asserts: "We need to learn what the immigrants' kids have so [that] we can bottle it and sell it, because many members of the African-American community, particularly among the chronically poor, have lost that sense of purpose and values which produced our generation" (*New York Times* 6/24/04).

First of all, like his tricky *Signifying Monkey Theory*, Gates evades the most significant and disturbing aspect of the problem; and it is the fact that these "immigrants' kids" are not just besting or excelling the "chronically poor" among the African-American community, they are also handily besting (or soundly beating) the very top, or cream, of the Black middle-class. Even so, Gates' *Manichaean pretense* is one that is deeply ingrained psychologically in the critic. One only needs to read his admittedly well-written autobiography titled *Colored People* to arrive at such conclusion. In this book, one finds the writer, rather gratuitously, attributing his literary and intellectual aptitude to the distaff (or mother's) side of the family. Not quite surprisingly, his distaff familial side is described as half-Irish and relatively more privileged. Skippy's mother is also the church secretary, which immediately pictures for the reader the seminal provenance of his esthetic and literary flair. In other words, Gates' mother is the familial intellectual while his stereotypically African father, the sawmill-worker, or some such blue-collar orderly, is the familial muscle—the proverbial Boxer of George Orwell's *Animal Farm*.

During the late 1980s, when he did not seem to feel quite comfortable with both his interracial marriage and his humble familial background, particularly on the agnatic (or father's side) of the family, Skip Gates used to joke about his father's inability to effectively pronounce or articulate certain standard English words—for instance, he would laugh at how his father would say "wif," instead of "with." One such occasion was during the august Langston Hughes Festival, hosted annually by the Department of English at the City College of New York, in 1989. On this occasion, Gates also mentioned the fact that many African-Americans who learned that he was married to a white woman, Sharon, or some such personality, a ceramist of some sort, were utterly flabbergasted. As to why these "indigenous" African-American people were flabbergasted was not quite clear to this writer; this is because even at the apogee of his fame and productivity, the man never quite projected himself as a vintage African-American. In fact, he unabashedly called himself a cultural and genetic hybrid. He also routinely made vitriolic remarks against the Afrocentrists; and, in fact, it was **hybrid intellectuals** like Skip Gates who convinced some right-wing white-Americans to equate the theory of Afrocentricity with Minister Louis Farrakhan's branch of the Nation of Islam. During the late 1980s and 1990s, for instance, Gates snobbishly portrayed the Afrocentrists, particularly the Temple University school spearheaded by Molefi Kete Asante, as a band of pseudo-scholars and pharaohs of a patently fabricated ancient African civilization.

That he should almost overnight convert himself into a **Feeding Bottle Theorist** is quite amusing. This is because anybody who has had the misfortune of either watching or reading Professor Gates' **Wonders of the African World** comes away totally convinced that there is virtually nothing worthwhile for any African-American to learn from his or her continental African kin. Interestingly and paradoxically, the man who kept insisting that the so-called sub-Saharan Africa had no viable culture and civilization throughout much of the ancient world, as well as the contemporary era, seemed to have finally learned a thing or two in his highly tendentious travelogue. When he visits the celebrated and venerable mosque at Timbuktu, Mali, and is shown a library full of books, largely penned by African scholars and philosophers, Gates rather sheepishly pretends that this is the very first time that any African-American, and American in general, is being let in on this open-secret. And yet, curiously enough, for more than four decades prior to his Timbuktu adventure, African-American autodidact scholars like John Henrik Clarke had written and lectured extensively on this subject. By 1994, or thereabouts, when he had become firmly established as mainstream America's Sony Liston, Professor Gates would scornfully resort to routinely branding the diligent and venerable likes of Professor John Henrik Clarke as pseudo-scholars, in such newspapers and magazines of record as **The New York Times** and **The New Yorker**.

It is also rather pathetic for Professor Henry Louis Gates, Jr., to be calling for the imperative need to "bottle and sell" whatever genie it is that has been assisting continental Africans and their African-Caribbean kin to handily best their African-American "distant relatives." Indeed, if he had been paying sedulous attention to his Black History classes at Yale University, assuming that he had possessed the requisite humility or self-will and self-love to motivate him to take such courses, Skip Gates would have learned more than three decades ago that as early as 1933, when his seminal Afrocentric classic was first published, Dr. Carter G. Woodson, a distinguished and pioneering Harvard University alumnus, was seriously questioning the kind of effete and thoroughly bankrupt curriculum that served as the basis of African-American education. In his *Mis-Education of the Negro*, Dr. Woodson urgently called for the kind of Black cultural irredentism, or constructive reclamation, that has been vigorously promoted by the likes of Maulana Karenga, J. Carruthers, Asa Hilliard and Molefi Kete Asante, which Mr. Gates spent most of the 1980s and 1990s systematically undermining. But, here again, one has to be a little charitable and honest to admit that the young Skip Gates initially endorsed the Afrocentric paradigm, but only to sadly dismiss it shortly thereafter, perhaps for some capriciously personal reasons. He had even reviewed Molefi Asante's *The Afrocentric Idea* and even written a blurb for this remarkable polemic piece. Interestingly, by 1995, Professor Gates had swung the proverbial pendulum one-hundred-and-eighty degrees in order to expediently label himself an Afrocentrist and, as was to be expected, appended with a well-calculated caveat to the effect that Gates was a different type of Afrocentrist, a more scholarly, objective and inclusive one, to be certain. During this period, this writer was teaching African History and African-American Studies at Indiana State University, Terre Haute, and could vividly remember Drs. Joseph Waxlemann and Keith Byerman expressing their utter consternation at such apparently overnight turnaround. For those of our readers who may not be familiar with the foregoing gentlemen, Dr. Joseph Waxlemann is the founding editor of the *Black Forum*, which later became *The African-American Review*, a journal that is sponsored by the Modern Language Association of America (MLA), the leading organization of humanities scholars and teachers in the United States. In 1995, while this writer taught at Indiana State University, as he also worked on his doctoral dissertation, Dr. Waxlemann was the dean of the college of arts and sciences. He was generally an urbane, erudite and a quite affable intellectual. Dr. Keith Byerman, who seemed to be quite reclusive and reticent but somewhat set in his Eurocentric ideological manners, for he insisted on calling Dr. W. E. B. DuBois an African-American instead of a legitimately naturalized citizen of Ghana. I had to remind these gentlemen, if memory serves us right, back then, that for Skip Gates such hefty ideological choices were far less about (one's) ethical convictions than the money (or greenback).

5

I don't know what Harvard University's Professors Lani Guinier and Henry Louis Gates, Jr., might think of the decision by the 2004 Democratic Party presidential nominee to select the child of a deceased East African immigrant by a white woman from Kansas as the keynoter for this year's Democratic National Convention, but in all likelihood this might, definitely, have come as utterly surprising. Or, perhaps, even outright disgusting. For Mr. Barack Obama describes himself as the son of a Kenyan scholarship student and a working class white-American, Mid-Western mother. Mr. Obama was born right here in the United States; however, going by the judgment of Professors Gates and Guinier, this 42-year-old Harvard Law School graduate does not yet qualify to be legally, or legitimately, designated an African-American. Unfortunately our subject, who is being given a stiff and jaundiced opposition by a self-described "descendant of slaves and cotton-pickers," in his well-deserved run for the United States senate out of the State of Illinois, rather "erroneously" describes himself as an African-American. The opponent, Dr. Alan Keyes, a perennial electoral upstart and impudent carpetbagger from the State of Maryland, claims that Mr. Obama, quite ironically, represents the opinions of ardent and erstwhile slavocrats, simply because the latter staunchly believes in the fundamental human right of an American woman to choose whether to have an abortion or not. "I would still be picking cotton if the country's moral principles had not been shaped by the Declaration of Independence," the Harvard-educated Mr. Keyes is quoted as saying (**African-American Observer** 8/17-23/04: 12). Actually, it is Mr. Keyes, a conservative Republican Party hack, who squarely represents the views of ardent racists and impudent slavocrats. For had he bothered to read a page or two of African-American history, the presumptuous **Afropean** would have learned to his utter horror that the admittedly egregious act of infanticide was routinely practiced by enslaved African-American mothers who did not want the future of their children to be rendered as apocalyptically bleak as their very own. Then again, who ever recognized Mr. Keyes as a critical thinker worthy of serious public attention or discourse?

In any case, for our renowned Ivy critics, to qualify for the cultural and political designation of African-American, one ought to be able to lead these self-appointed *racial authenticators* (or are they commissioners?) to the moorings of an ancestor who was once a slave here in the United States, particularly in one of the Southern states. Failure to do so ineluctably implies that Mr. Barack Obama could only contend himself with being disdainfully classified as an "immigrant's kid." Indeed, the latter is patently, according to the ***Gatesian-Guinierian Test of Racial Authenticity***, some aberrant sort of unbranded quadruped or animal; in brief, the establishment of Mr. Obama's humanity has yet to be determined. And this is, undoubtedly, far into the future, perhaps, umpteen generations hence. Our Harvard critics do not specify just exactly how many generations "the kid of an immigrant," particularly an African and an African-Caribbean "kid," is to qualify for U. S. citizenship. Of course, there is one quite daunting ***Grandfather's Clause*** demanded by the ***Gatesian-Guinierian Test of Racial Authenticity*** that Mr. Obama almost certainly could never meet; and it is that all of his grandparents ought to have been born right here in the United States, the failure of which he is almost guaranteed to be compelled to return any assistance that Mr. Obama might have received from Harvard University under the aegis of good, old Affirmative Action.

There is one aspect of his humanity, unfortunately, that the ***Gatesian-Guinierian Test of Racial Authenticity*** does not address; and it is the fact that our subject has a white mother, the same as Ms. Guinier. But, of course, Ms. Guinier stands over and far above her own racial authenticity test. For the children of interracial Africans and African-Caribbeans, as well as to some unspecified degree African-Americans, are also a part of the new scapegoats of perceived Black under-achievement in "the most selective" American colleges and universities. And since whites are en-mass and indisputably classified as ***oppressors*** by virtually every traditional ***race-warrior***, it is quite certain that the likes of Mr. Obama are in very deep trouble, simply for allowing their ***zebra*** selves, apologies to Sherman Helmsley, to be born right here in these United States. And to top off his abject effrontery, one that almost verges on the blasphemous, Mr. Barack Obama is running as a Democratic senatorial candidate from Illinois, where he practices as a civil rights attorney, a crackerjack attorney, we have learned. Needless to say, it would come as no surprise, at all, if these Harvard kingpins decide to launch a massive ***Stop-Obama*** campaign during the run-up to the November 2004 general election. Alas, there is a glaring contradiction here—Professor Guinier is of mixed-race ancestry: her mother is white and Jewish, we understand. But as has already been established, Ms. Guinier, the first African-American woman professor to be tenured by the king-makers of Harvard Law School, stands over and far above the ***Gatesian-Guinierian Test of Racial Authenticity***.

Being a pioneer, it goes without saying, has its own capricious privileges; and this is why many of America's European-born Founding Fathers could confidently and comfortably enshrine in the august Constitution of the United States that after they had passed on the political landscape, any future would-be-president ought to, perforce, have been born in the United States of America.

On the other hand, Professor Gates, as we adumbrated earlier on, is married to a white woman called Sharon (not to be confused with the current Prime Minister of the State of Israel); the couple met, legend has it, at the *Newsweek* magazine a little over twenty years ago. They were both cub-reporters, or it appears that Mrs. Gates was a staff photographer, or some such staffer. Like Ms. Guinier's mother, Mrs. Sharon Gates is also Jewish; her exact extraction or nationality is not quite clear. And if memory serves readers right, Mr. Gates dedicated his putative magnum opus, *The Signifying Monkey*, to Mrs. Sharon Gates. The latter book, for which "distant relative" Skippy went on to clinch the coveted Mac-Arthur Foundation's Genius Award, is about African-American literary theory—it is actually about diasporic Black orature or oral literature, though the brazenly Panglossian Professor Gates glibly presumes his *Signifying Monkey* to amply address the rather complex and diverse sensibilities of continental African literary artists. And Professor Gates is not very well-known as a champion of any continental African cause or causes. For as already hinted, the entire thrust of his *Wonders of the African World* was to depict continental Africans, particularly those of the so-called sub-Saharan Africa, as immutable savages and abject slavocrats. Mr. Gates never quite musters the courage to honestly admit that not every African who was deported into the Americas was an innocent victim of an egregious and flagrant human traffic, what some distinguished white-American liberal historians have labeled *The Peculiar Institution*. Of course, this patently established historical fact in no way or manner meliorates the continental African portion, or role, in this bizarrely protracted transaction. In his sterling presentation to the Democratic Party Convention in Boston, and the nation at large, Mr. Barack Obama poignantly noted that his own father had been a cattle-herdboy in Kenya prior to his emigration into the United States, some forty years ago, as a scholarship student. His grandfather, who appears to have had a phantasmagoric imagination on the order of the Empire State Building or, better yet, the Statue of Liberty, had been a domestic cook to the extant British colonialists in Kenya. So Mr. Obama is one whose ancestors knew and almost certainly experienced something not very far removed from America's *Peculiar Institution*. But, of course, the rubrics of the *Gatesian-Guinierian Racial Authenticity Test* proscribes such excruciating experience. It did not occur right here in the United

States. And in the ***wondrous*** imagination of Professor Gates, all Africans, without exceptions, are impudent slavocrats and cultural barbarians. And, of course, as the entire world knows, we are very proud in our barbarism. In fact, it was this bestial aspect of continental Africans which Dr. Gates sought to emphasize to the civilized worlds of America's PBS-TV and the BBC when he visited Cape Coast Castle and cornered some well-meaning but apparently grossly ill-informed African-Americans and forced them to admit that Cape Coast and, by extension, Ghana were no Meccas but bona fide Auschwitzes for African-Americans. It did not help matters that Skip Gates also encountered a tourist guide who was too camera-crazy and intellectually callow to have readily caught onto the celebrated wiles of our African-American ***Kwaku Ananse***. Our "distant cousin," of course.

Needless to say, the Obama story is one that continental Africans are indescribably proud to make their own, all vicious and pathetic attempts by the ***Gatesian-Guinierian Theorists*** and fanatics to the contrary notwithstanding.

6

The Gatesian-Guinierian debate on the need for Ivy League institutions to drastically reduce the remarkable presence of continental African and African-Caribbean undergraduates at the aforementioned academies is rather bizarre and grossly misguided. For it glibly presumes that every non-American born—or first-generation—Black person gained admission into these "selective" colleges and universities on the crest of Affirmative Action, or by simply playing the proverbial *race-card*. Nothing could be farther from the truth. To be certain, long before both Professors Gates and Guinier, and their ideological disciples, dreamed of attending Yale and Harvard universities, or any of the other Ivy League institutions, for that matter, a countless number of continental Africans and Caribbeans had already graduated from these institutions with flying colors, as it were.

In Nigeria, for instance, we had late President Nnamdi Azikiwe, who graduated from the Columbia University School of Journalism long before Mr. Gates was even conceived; and in Ghana, we had President Kwame Nkrumah, the man who is widely credited with having engineered the establishment of the discipline of African Studies at flagship universities, or academies, here in the United States. Later, we would have scholars and educators like Professor Gyandoh, of Temple University, a legal luminary and former dean of the University of Ghana Law School. Professor Gyandoh is a Yale Law School graduate, just like Professor Kofi Asare Opoku, a leading theorist of traditional African religions, who obtained a Master of Theological Studies degree from the very institution out of which Skip Gates earned his Bachelor of Arts degree in History; and then more than two generations before the "Signifying Monkey Theorist" obtained his doctorate from Cambridge University, Mr. William (Paa Willie) Ofori-Atta, one of this writer's granduncles, had earned degrees in Law and Economics from that world-renowned academy.

Here in the United States, this writer's elder brother would earn a doctoral degree in Nuclear Physics from Columbia University, nearly about the same time that Skip Gates was at Cambridge reading African and African-American Literature. The former, it is significant to recall, had obtained both his Bachelor's and Master's degrees from Columbia University. And here, also, it must be loudly emphasized that my brother did not enter Columbia University under an Affirmative Action largesse, as these critics might be tempted to presume. In fact, in 1976, my brother scored the highest mark or grade on the SAT in the entire African continent, thereby being awarded a full-scholarship to attend New York State's oldest and most prestigious academy. And not very long ago, my brother obtained his second Doctorate in Computer Science from the Ivy network system. I, on the other hand, made the personal decision not to apply to or attend any Ivy League institution, shortly after learning that the history of the Ivy League had little or nothing to do with scholarship but sports and games!

The preceding notwithstanding, while the significance of an Ivy imprimatur cannot be overemphasized, for the continental African, unlike his or her diasporic African kin, a diploma, or certificate, from a good college or university is more important than simply one from an Ivy League academy. And to be certain, this ideological suasion or thrust has been partially the source of sibling dissension between this writer and his elder brother. The Ivy League, as famous African-American scholar Carter G. Woodson, a Harvard graduate, recognized more than three generations ago, has a bizarre way of making the alumnus feel an unsavory and quite unproductive sense of self-importance. And the preceding is what I have always sought to point out to my American students, Black and white. For until very recently, continental Africans put more value on culture and familial affiliation or background as the defining parameters of one's identity and place in society, rather than merely the college which one attended. This, however, is not to suggest that higher educational achievement was not respected—former South African president Nelson R. Mandela made this patently clear shortly after his widely publicized release from Robben Island's maximum security prison. It is just that traditional societies value good social conduct much more than the mere acquisition of book knowledge and marketable professional skills. A doctoral degree from Duke University, for instance, would not guarantee the holder easy access to the august Asante monarchy, as Skip Gates himself attested in his filmic documentary titled "Wonders of the African World." Rather, any degree from a good academy or university ought to be aptly coupled with the holder's remarkable respect for his or her elders, as well as one's socioeconomic and cultural subordinates, in order to be deemed valid or worthwhile.

In fine, continental Africans believe in what leading Kenyan political scientist Professor Ali A. Mazrui terms as "the social responsibility of scholarship." If, indeed, Uncle Skippy is serious about his search for any African academic genie to bottle and sell to his disciples, as he has called for, this is precisely where to begin. Interestingly, it is also on this score that we vehemently disagree with the chairman of Harvard University's Department of African-American Studies that the apparently, relatively lackluster performance of "indigenous" African-Americans vis-à-vis their recent immigrant African kin is hardly "because many members of the African-American community, particularly among the chronically poor, have lost their sense of purpose and [the] values which produced our [i.e. Gates'] generation" (*New York Times* 6/24/04). Rather, what the Keyser, West Virginia-native ought to be asking of himself and his peers is why their generation woefully failed to effectively transmit, or pass onto the younger generation, the kind of sense of purpose and cultural values that made the Gatesian-Guinierian generation as successful as it both claims and appears to be. Needless to say, the answer, in Shakespearean parlance, lies not in our stars but squarely within ourselves. And by the preceding we imply, as the great traditional Akan-Ghanaian thinkers aptly maintained, that a crab does not bring forth a bird. In sum, the perceived failure of our youth, assuming that such assertion has any validity, reflects the logical failure of the older generation.

We also expect Professor Gates to have a remarkable sense of the cause of the perceived relative under-performance of "indigenous" African-Americans vis-à-vis their continental and African-Caribbean kin or counterparts, being that he obtained his doctoral degree from a flagship British academy, in fact, the first African-American to do so at Cambridge University. And here, we vividly recall Dr. Gates himself woefully lamenting in the introduction to one of his books—"Figures in Black"?—that his highly coveted Yale University undergraduate degree in History had not adequately prepared him for the kind of sterling writing and critical thinking skills required at Cambridge. And guess what? It was the same dons and faculty at renowned and elite institutions like Cambridge and Oxford who helped to establish such world-renowned continental African academies as the universities of Ghana, Ibadan and Makerere, among a host of others. And so why is there any reason for Professors Guinier and Gates to pretend that continental Africans are not supposed to be out-performing their African-American kin? And, to be certain, if these seemingly perplexed critics were really serious about finding a constructive solution to their problem, they would also have realized that continental African students are also out-performing white, Latin and Asian Americans! The grim paradox, however, inheres in the fact that this bleak state of affairs comes at a time during which the United States is the sole superpower nation on earth.

For those of us who have been studiously observing the American political landscape over the past generation, however, this harrowing state of affairs comes as hardly any surprise. Our leaders in Washington, particularly those of the

Republican-wing of our republic, no pun intended, prefer to expend our hard-earned dollars and cents shadow-boxing with purported terrorist organizations and personalities. Education is no longer a top national priority, it seems; and it is not even clear whether it ever was in these United States of America.

7

There are too many good African-Americans doing great works and undertaking constructive ventures and projects in continental Africa and the Caribbean; and so when we are called upon by some pathologically cynical Black intellectuals and educators to justify our humanity and presence here in the United States, particularly our presence at some of the most elite of this country's academies, it becomes quite a Herculean task. For how does one effectively defend oneself and one's people against another portion of the same group? Apparently, Professors Henry Louis Gates, Jr., and Lani Guinier do not appreciate the foregoing fact. And the fact is that fundamentally speaking, no reasonably well-educated or intelligent African sees her-or himself as different from his or her diasporic African kin. The preceding notwithstanding, when such deviously puerile attempt at dividing global African people comes from the Henry Louis Gateses of this world, it is not entirely surprising. For in spite of his remarkable command of his academic sub-discipline of African-American Literature, the Keyser (or is it Piedmont?), West Virginia, native remains very much an acutely conflicted personality and has remained so for at least the last two decades.

During the 1980s, for instance, when he was a rising star and in hot demand and pursuit by many a mainstream American academy, Mr. Gates wrote and lectured extensively about his firm belief in the total absence of any racial experience here in America, particularly, and the world in general. Back then he emphatically labeled the ideological and cultural concept of *race* as purely "a state of mind." In other words, for Gates, the objective and empirical, or historical, African-American experience did not exist as such; it was patently or wholly a figment of woefully distorted sensibilities. Consequently, Skip Gates furiously and contemptuously began to label *Afrocentric theories* and such radical African-American intellectuals and activists as Malcolm X, Maulana Karenga, Jacob Carruthers and Asa Hilliard as *essentialists*. Professor Gates' Ghanaian-British colleague Anthony Kwame Appiah offered the former considerable boost. And here, it may be significantly recalled that both Gates and Appiah met at Cambridge University during the late 1970s and struck up a friendship that appears to have survived until now. Professor Appiah specializes in Western Philosophy, though he has expended much of his formidable intellectual capital in systematically undermining the culture and philosophy of his patrilineage, the Akan-Asante nation of Ghana. This widely acknowledged relative of Queen Elizabeth II does not appear to harbor any modicum of respect for the Asante people, particularly the latter's monarch, whatsoever, for some capriciously personal reasons which he adumbrates in his book titled *In My Father's House*. In the latter book, which was awarded the Melville Herskovitz Prize by the predominantly white African Studies Association of the United States, in 1993, Professor Appiah sneers when bound for advanced studies at Cambridge, his erudite father exhorts him to uphold the family tradition. He questions himself as to whether his father's family possessed any authentic scholastic tradition, by Western standards, requiring upholding. And here also, it is significant to observe that unlike Skip Gates' father who was a factory hand, Anthony Kwame Appiah's father, Mr. Joseph (Joe) Appiah, was a very distinguished Ghanaian lawyer. In fact the elder Appiah's death, during the early 1990s, attracted a wide coverage in the *New York Times*. The obituary was equally significant, both in view of the elder Appiah's genius as a legal scholar-practitioner, as well as a mercurial politician, as it was for the fact that he was perhaps the first African and Blackman to have married into the upper echelons of British society.

In Ghana, on the other hand, the elder Mr. Appiah was called or nicknamed *Political Chameleon*, largely because like Harvard University's David Gergen, the former had served in almost every government since his country's re-attainment of political independence from Britain, in 1957, without little or no regard for ideological persuasion or thrust. Naturally, the younger Mr. Appiah pays his father glowing tribute, even describing Uncle Joe as, perhaps, the most altruistic and forthright Ghanaian legal scholar and practitioner. Those who dubbed him a political chameleon, however, believe that the elder Mr. Appiah's quick-silver negotiation through the equally labile corridors of Ghanaian politics was largely about the money, as it were. Ardent Nkrumahists, including this writer's late father, for example, also called "Nationalist Joe" a traitor. And, in fact, the latter was once incarcerated by Prime Minister Nkrumah for what was then given as "the interest of national security." During the 1950s and '60s, such description could have encapsulated the unsavory practice of *micro-nationalism*, otherwise called *tribalism*. For "Nationalist Joe" had abruptly defected to join the Asante-dominated opposition to the Nkrumah government.

When Professor Gates speaks of race as a state of mind, it is not quite clear exactly what the renowned staff writer for *The New Yorker* magazine implies. He may merely be echoing the mainstream and largely pedestrian assertion of race as a social construct; which is perfectly a matter of common sense. The problem, however, arises when Professor Gates uses this objective fact to muffle, as well as muzzle up, the socio-cultural and political realities of racism which, by the way, is also an *essentialist* ideology ratified and practiced by the government of the United States with impunity, and thus the necessary enactment of Civil Rights and Affirmative Action legislation as political correctives. But it is also interesting to observe, at this juncture, that the Gatesian concept or ideology of race as a state of mind is not predicated upon sheer ignorance; for the Yale University alumnus is indisputably among the vanguard of the most knowledgeable and articulate African-American intellectuals. It is, therefore, incontrovertibly a matter of dollars and cents. For this pseudo-theory or ideology was advanced in the heat of the culture wars of the 1980s, when white conservatives in the Reagan-Bush government needed a Black proxy, or poster-boy, to do their dirty work of systematically undermining African-American progress. In fact, it was during this period that some of his peers in the academy began calling Skip Gates the "Booker-Tee" of the mainstream academy. Needless to say, Uncle Skippy would vehemently deny the charge and rather insist that he was arduously about the missionary business of building an enviable guild of Dr. DuBois' proverbial Talented Tenth.

And, indeed, there exists ample evidence of the latter. In 1993, for instance, during the annual conference of the African Studies Association, Professor Gates dispatched scouts to Boston's Westin Hotel—if memory serves this writer accurately—seeking to lure students away from Professor Molefi Kete Asante's African-American Studies department at Temple University. This writer was personally approached by a Ghanaian journalist who was then visiting as a fellow of the Kennedy School of Government. The scout suggested to me that the kind of Afrocentric theory being espoused at Temple University lacked bread-and-butter, or monetary, value. In other words, I would become more marketable if I left Temple and enrolled in such an august academic citadel as Harvard. I promptly retorted that while as an impecunious African the foregoing suggestion made a lot of sense, nevertheless, I was not quite ready to morph into a Dr. Faustus. The following day, at the aforementioned conference, the Ghanaian-journalist-turned-scout avoided this writer, either out of shame or anger, or a mixture of both. Indeed, Mr. Coomson was quite right to some extent. For today, I learn that my dear countryman is a filthily rich newspaper publisher, while I continue to perform budgetary acrobatics week in and out. Still, I make bold to assert that I am all the spiritually and psychically better for my flat refusal to compromise my dignity and human values. For, in retrospect, it is almost certain that Professor Gates would have written to inform me, after all, of his summary withdrawal of my diploma; for I am not an "indigenous" African-American in his estimation.

8

Many ardent African nationalists, both on the primeval continent, as it were, and the Diaspora, literally went up in arms in the wake of Professor Henry Louis Gates, Jr's *Wonders of the African World*, a three-part travelogue. The main grievance of these critics bordered on the vapidly shallow treatment of the historiography of Africa over the past five-hundred years. The preceding was more of an ideological pretense or gimmickry, as viewers and readers soon began to realize. The sole aim of the narrator appeared to be the unsparing depiction of continental Africans as morons and irredeemable or pathological slavocrats.

Fortunately, this well-financed travelogue—and one may aptly add, travesty—was shortly to fall flat on its prats, as it were. And the rather imperious narrator-author also woefully exposed his proverbial flanks, which was the grim fact that whatever the West Virginian native knew about Africa appeared to have been largely gleaned from cartoon characters. And that, indeed, was the salient reason behind the call of his most ardent and vociferous critics for Mr. Gates to have critically studied, before hand, Alex Haley's epic series *Roots*, which quite effectively attempted to put a human face on African history from an Afrocentric perspective.

And to be certain, while nobody seemed to doubt whether the proud Harvard University lecturer had amply familiarized himself with Mr. Haley's yeoman's contribution to global African history, almost all of his critics concurred that Mr. Gates had either totally misunderstood it or simply ignored *Roots'* critical implications for global humanity. For in the view of the Harvard jersey-sporting narrator of *Wonders of the African World*, the problem with continental Africans was their immutable African identity. It appeared to him that Africans could hardly do any better than be themselves, as envisioned by Aryan supremacist ideology—which is to be reckoned as the veritable scum of the human species.

On the preceding score, however, it is quite facilely tempting to conclude that Gatesian animosity is squarely and solely geared towards continental Africans. Such assessment is almost bound to be reckoned as at best simplistic and sophomoric—for the man is far more sophisticated in his calculated hatred for things non-Aryan than many of his critics and detractors would like to publicly admit. On the personal level, he has been monikered "a trickster-par-excellence" by some of those who do not like him but are in such unnerving awe of his purportedly scholastic genius as to be morbidly afraid of confronting him head-on. And by the label of "trickster," these critics and detractors—for some simply hate the man *ad hominem*—imply that the Yale and Oxbridge alumnus tends to brazenly project his personal insecurities onto those who are bold enough to buck the proverbial *system*. Such tendency is seen to border on jaundice or envy, as was recently witnessed during the annual conference of the Black alumni of Harvard University, during which Professors Gates and Guinier called for the academic and professional excision of continental African and African-Caribbean students from America's putative flagship academy. The irony is that among some members of the African-American academic community, Henry Louis Gates, Jr., is regarded as an *institution*, as one of this writer's professors, who also happens to be a Yale alumnus, once described his younger humanities idol. And if, indeed, he is an "institution," then the logical implication here is that Mr. Gates represents the very essence of indisputable merit, almost the diametrical opposite of *Brown versus Board of Education*, the latter's diachronic implications, that is. And, indeed, as Mr. Anthony Carnevale, a former vice president of the renowned Educational Testing Service, the fabricators of the SAT tests, aptly pointed out, good colleges are more interested in admitting "high-performing black students from immigrant families," rather than simply serving as the unreflective *Santa Claus* of people who cynically gloat on the grim and psychologically demoralizing fact of a slavocratic past or heritage.

The preceding, however, is not to imply that one's bleak and unsavory past ought to be totally ignored; only God knows how the global Jewish community has capitalized on its slavocratic past to empower it, to the enviable extent that this numerical minority, by virtue of its collective intellectual and economic prowess, is no longer reckoned an ethnic minority here in the United States. Rather, it is the nugatory tendency—or propensity—towards inordinately *essentializing* oppression as an academic requisite, as Professors Gates and Guinier appear to be doing, that ought to be unreservedly condemned. And here, also, it may be of great interest to point out that a remarkable number of continental Africans admitted to the "most selective colleges and universities" here in the United States come from economic backgrounds that are invariably bleaker than those of Black America's "chronically poor," whose inviolable cause Professors Gates and Guinier pretend to be championing. And if, indeed, their sole concern is socioeconomic equity, rather than the gratuitous exclusion of African and African-Caribbean immigrants, then their concern appears to be grossly misdirected. For, the perennial under-representation of "indigenous" African-Americans, who make up roughly 13-percent of America's population, in elite academic institutions, does not appear to be the logical outcome of having highly-motivated immigrant continental African and African-Caribbean children in remarkable numbers at these institutions. Rather, it is almost squarely the result of the abject failure on the part of mainstream America to provide unfettered academic access to the children of "indigenous" African-Americans, in order to ensure that the latter are able to readily compete with not only the children of Black immigrants, but also the equally highly-motivated children of Asians, Latin-Americans and European immigrants.

It would also be interesting to learn from Professors Guinier and Gates just how the deleterious impact of racism might, indeed, have considerably restricted the otherwise remarkable presence of Black immigrant children's access to these highly selective institutions. For, here again, these critics and detractors cannot pretend or seriously deny the objective reality of anti-African racism and outright hatred here in the United States. And such unprovoked animosity, it is interesting to note, has been meted by both white-Americans and their "indigenous" African-American compatriots. And here, also, it goes without saying that there are remarkable exceptions.

As for the implications of having "indigenous" African-Americans continually under-represented in the most selective academic and professional institutions, the question is one of leadership. About seven years ago, Professor Gates co-authored a book titled *The Future of the Race* with Dr. Cornel West. The latter book was reviewed by this writer in the *New York Amsterdam News*, indisputably a leading newspaper of record in Black America. Unfortunately, the review was garbled by the printers and editors of the aforementioned newspaper, a frequent and routine practice, perhaps for spatial reasons. In sum, if memory serves this writer accurately, the thesis of the co-authors of *The Future of the Race* did not even remotely suggest anything to the effect that the purportedly highly-motivated children of continental African immigrants were squarely to blame for the apparently bleak political destiny of Black America, as Professor Gates appears now to suggest. Rather, the call went out for an imperative ideological redirection, from reactionary to proactive leadership.

9

When Dr. Henry Louis Gates, Jr., asks the question: "What are the implications [of the highly-motivated children of continental African immigrants besting their "indigenous" African-American counterparts in Ivy League institutions]?" he almost prompts those of us who have been studiously following his career during the course of the last two decades to guffaw, or break out with uncontrollable laughter. This is because once the renowned critic reduces this highly pervasive, cross-economic or class-transcending problematic to a simple matter of "the chronically poor [having] lost that sense of purpose and values which produced [the Gatesian] generation" (**New York Times** 6/24/04), he immediately produces a contradiction in terms; for the children of the "chronically poor" among "indigenous" African-Americans cannot be synched with the indubitably ideological and academic concept of "highly motivated [and] self-selected group[s]" of continental African and African-Caribbean immigrant children. For the former ascription designates a more complex issue of geopolitical milieu, whereas the latter primarily alludes to familial and personal cultures, something that is largely attitudinal, more of a learned or acquired behavior than one that is either circumstantial or political.

And on this score, matters get even more interesting, for Professor Gates, as one also presumes the same to be for Professor Guinier, Africans and African-Americans are fundamentally two discrete groups of people. They may share a common historical provenance or background, but for Mr. Gates this commonality is so remote as to be virtually irrelevant; it is simply the stuff of epic mythology, the sort of material that might be occasionally used in the same manner that, for instance, the ancestry of modern Italians is tangentially traced to the ancient Greeks and the Romans. Which is why when he was asked by a Public Television (PBS-TV) network executive how he envisaged continental Africans, Professor Gates promptly and almost contemptuously called us his "distant relatives," and nothing more or less.

And so whether the perceivedly relative under-representation of "indigenous" African-Americans has any "implications," or ramifications, for either group of the human species is not quite clear. Mr. Gates himself does not specify this, though one can readily surmise from his patently alarmist attitude that the

Oxbridge schooled West Virginian sees continental Africans in the shape and form of parasitic intruders, what Americans disdainfully term as "freeloaders." In **Coetzeean** terminology, there is an invasion of the purported turf of Black Americans by continental African barbarians. And this conclusion is no figment of this writer's poetic imagination; for although he has never attended any of the so-called highly selective American colleges and universities, he has been meted the kind of roughshod treatment that Professor Gates and Guinier appear to have in mind for the children of continental African immigrants and their African-Caribbean kin. Indeed, Mr. Gates cannot pretend that his rather extortionate and outright callous call for the measured excision of "non-indigenous" African-Americans is one of sheer polemic or argumentation. For like Ralph Ellison, an admittedly great American novelist, Professor Gates sees only "color" as the sole ethnological linkage between African-Americans and Africans. This may largely explain why his autobiography was titled "Colored People." In the latter book, published in the 1990s, Mr. Gates strains to erase his African identity; at best, he sees himself as a cultural hybrid. The author is a bona fide Irish-American with a blameless great-grandfather called Mr. Gates (or is it Lord Gates?), and a nondescript African slave great-grandmother who does not have any remarkable ethnic identity besides the fact that she is introduced in order to make for a good story.

Indeed, the bleak academic portrait painted by Professors Guinier and Gates transcends the Ivy Corridors, as it were. The fact has remained over the last two decades that more African-American males are wont to land in prison cells than in any other kind of degree-awarding institution, "selective" or "non-selective." And thus to pretend that it is only a Harvard or Yale education, rather than simply a good education, that would land one a respectable niche or premium socio-economic position in America's "inner circles of power"—whatever this means—is simply preposterous. In brief, this is just another impudent way, or means, for Professor Gates to announce to the Black American world that he has arrived at the very pinnacle of the mainstream American academy. And, on this score, we heartily and unreservedly congratulate him for his enviable achievement. But we also quizzically recognize that the Keyser, West Virginia native abhors the ineluctable fact that he should be sharing his laurels with the likes of Emmanuel Akyeampong, Kwame Anthony Appiah and Orlando Patterson, among a host of other "non-indigenous" Africans and African-Caribbeans.

It is also quite interesting to learn that Professor Gates has spent much of the past two decades, or so, depicting Nation of Islam (NOI) chief minister Louis Farrakhan as an inveterate white-hating Black man. Now it appears that birds of the same feathers are flocking together, as it were. And here also, it is significant to emphasize that we do not in any way imply that Minister Louis Farrakhan is in any shape or form a white-hating Black man. This morally grave judgment call belongs to the proverbial American white man and his woman. And while we may not exactly concur with much of his diatribe against the so-called mainstream America, we, nevertheless, appreciate the fact that the NOI leader has done far more to constructively champion the cause of global Africans than both Professors Gates and Guinier could ever boast of. And whether his apparent contempt for the NOI leader stems from the fact of the latter's African-Caribbean ancestry, is one that has to be determined by readers and critics. And who, between Professor Gates and Minister Farrakhan, is the worse for such lurid conniption? Needless to say, here, again, we reserve any judgment for readers and critics, as well as posterity.

Indeed, attempting to distinguish continental Africans from their so-called indigenous African-American kin may not be nearly as simple as Professors Gates and Guinier appear to believe. For instance, how would these Harvard intellectuals categorize the children of recent immigrants from such Anglo-American, slavo-colonial satellite countries as Sierra Leone and Liberia? Professors Gates and Guinier also seem to equate Affirmative Action with racial entitlement, rather than as a merit-based program aimed at meliorating the deleterious impact of de facto and de jure racism in the admissions process into "the most selective" academies. And then for Mr. Gates to ask: "What are the implications [of having more continental African immigrants' children enrolled in the best American colleges and universities] for "indigenous" African-Americans?" reminds one of that jaded Jehovah's Witness joke which predicted the end of the world, or the Apocalypse, to occur in 1980. And here, we may also be apt to ask: "What have been the implications of having more Asian, Latin-American and European immigrants' children in the finest American educational institutions than we have had continental African children and their African-Caribbean kin?" Indeed, what Professors Gates and Guinier may not be aware of, or care to know, is that the very remarkable trend regarding the rise in the merit-based presence of continental Africans and Caribbeans in the most elite institutions is also being duplicated in Britain and various parts of Western Europe. And here, also, we mention Britain because it is even far more difficult to gain admission into such time-honored and prestigious institutions as Cambridge, Oxford, Leeds and London than most of the Ivy League academies here in the United States. And what is even more intriguing, these Africans and Caribbeans are not entering such august institutions on the crest of Affirmative Action, at least not formally.

In one of his books or articles, Professor Gates recalls his initial encounter with his longtime British-Ghanaian friend Dr. Kwame Anthony Appiah and wonders how it would feel to have the names of one's ancestors grace majestic buildings and hallways on an Oxbridge campus. Dr. Appiah's mother, Peggy Appiah, it may be recalled, is a close kin of Queen Elizabeth II. The former's father was leader of the British Labor Party during the 1950s. And here, we make note of the fact that the preceding is being recalled to emphasize what we have been maintaining all along, that much of his anti-African diatribe reflects Mr. Gates' own personal inadequacies, his meteoric and phenomenal achievements notwithstanding. You see, I or nobody that I know went to school or college wondering about how it felt to have one's ancestor or a grandparent's name etched on a building, instead of concentrating on our studies. This was not because none of our grandparents had distinguished themselves in their generation or age (God knows many of them had more than acquitted themselves), just that for us the mere privilege or opportunity for the acquisition of a good education was simply enough.

10

There is one genie that Professors Gates and Guinier may want to bottle and sell to their disciples if, indeed, they staunchly believe that the relatively greater presence of continental Africans and their African-Caribbean kin at "the most selective" institutions, purportedly at the damnable expense of "indigenous" African-Americans, need or ought to be promptly reversed. It is the pervasive climate or attitude of anti-intellectualism among many an African-American youth or youngster. And if one may vividly recall, Skip Gates has himself in the past written about this disturbing state of affairs, the curious notion that academic and intellectual pursuits and achievements are the exclusive or especial preserves of white-Americans. This regressive attitude is not without historical provenance—the umpteen generations and centuries during which the Diasporic African was forcibly kept out of and away from all venues and avenues of civilized, modern culture, except as a cog in the primitive advancement of Western technology and society.

Interestingly, however, this harrowing experience was not peculiar to the Western Blackman, as it were; it equally impacted the mundane and diurnal existence of the continental African. But the latter had one advantage over the former, the fact that whatever excruciating experiences s/he encountered occurred in his or her own polity or geocultural environment. For the psychologically traumatizing experience that came with massive African deportation and enslavement in the so-called Americas cannot be overemphasized. And so when we herein affirm that we know of almost no continental Africans or African-Caribbeans inhabiting their respective polities who religiously believe that intellectual achievement is tantamount to "acting white," as one routinely encounters in the Harlems and Bedstuys of inner-city America, such observation is made with utmost humility and sensitivity, notwithstanding the fact of its absolute unacceptability.

The preceding maugre, if, indeed, Professors Gates and Guinier care to know, remarkable numbers of the "immigrant kids" from Africa and the Caribbean who live and socialize among their "indigenous" African-American peers and kin have also quite surprisingly, but not wholly unexpectedly, imbibed this psychologically emasculating ideology. And here, we speak far less in terms of theory than inductive realities. Indeed, a blistering case in point is this writer's eldest niece, an otherwise brilliant young woman, who quickly resorted to the indiscriminate use of **Ebonics**—or Black English (call it Black-speak or Black-speech)—shortly after immigrating into the United States some twelve years ago. My niece was particularly fond of the use of double negatives and such routine abuse of tenses as: "I had went"; "I did it already" and "I had did it." And whenever her maternal uncle brought this unsavory linguistic attitude to her attention, particularly its economic and political implications, or drawbacks, his niece would simply sneer and retort that she wasn't going to be whitewashed by anybody, and that her uncle could take his cultural elitism somewhere else.

I emphasize the fact that I am the maternal uncle of Nana Afua Birago, because among the Akan of Ghana one's maternal uncle is invariably, and ineluctably, the most important and powerful male figure in a niece's or nephew's life. This avuncular role, unfortunately, is rapidly dying out, largely the logical consequence of acute Westernization and the morally atrophying individualism that comes with such alien and alienating experience. This hitherto imperious position of the maternal uncle in a polygynous culture tended to remarkably offset paternal irresponsibility. There are several genetic, cultural and philosophical or ideological factors that ensured the imperious role of a maternal uncle in a niece's or nephew's life. Even in non-matrilineal cultures, where a father's brother assumed the role of primary guardian, to a lesser degree, the effect was very much the same. These guardians buffered up the deleterious and not infrequent dereliction of one's paternity, a salutary practice that is sorely lacking in urbanized Black America for purely historical and political reasons but which, with constructive leadership will and parental determination could be revived in one form or another. And to be certain, those who grew up in the Plantation South, as it were, where African-American culture maintains its closest affinity with much of its continental African counterparts, would readily attest to this fact. And so what appears to be uniquely and intractably African-American is in reality globally African. And for those among us who adamantly tout the uniqueness of the proverbial African-American experience, one only needs to examine the apocalyptic slavo-colonial experiences of Africans in the Congo, Angola, Mozambique and South Africa, among others, in order to sober up and get off their proverbial high horses.

At the end of the day, increasingly, as continental Africans and their African-Caribbean kin rapidly assimilate into the larger and general African-American population, for our kind of institutionally racist society would have it no other way, these so-called recent immigrants, in Gatesian-Guinierian parlance **pariahs**, are also increasingly meeting with the same fate as their "indigenous" or "more native" (or autochthonous), if there is any such phenomenon, kin. For it is an indubitably or patently established fact that the raging Hip-Hop culture, which the luminary likes of Cornel West and Michael Eric Dyson have extensively written about, is the brainchild of the children of African-Caribbean immigrants, as Skip Gates disdainfully depicts them. And regarding the story of my niece, today, Nana Afua Birago is a 22-year-old mother without a bachelor's degree, the immutable minimum of academic and professional qualification required by a continental African, or a "non-indigenous" African-American, to succeed here in the United States. It is also rather sad to have to recall that Nana, a multi-talented young woman, attended one of the finest secondary schools—St. Rose's—in Ghana and creditably acquitted herself by earning the equivalent of 10 "A's," out of the 11 courses that she studied. As I write this piece, I am on my way to Worcester, Massachusetts, to wistfully participate in the "outdooring" (or Christening) ceremonies for my first grandniece, Leah Afua Gyamfuaa. And the fact that the latter's granduncle turned forty-one not very long ago, is something to think about. I don't know what the well-meaning reader might make of this fact; for my part, I am firmly convinced that I am far too young to become a granduncle. That is not to say, or even imply, however, that I am not elated by the experience, because I definitely am. On another level also, this is not quite my maiden experience, particularly when one reckons these affairs from the integral perspective of the traditional African extended family structure. To be certain, my oldest known cousin is Mr. Samuel Nicholas Kwadwo Adu, a former West African table-tennis (or Ping-Pong) champion (during the 1950s), who is 72 years old, almost the age of Skip Gates' own parents. My siblings and I, however, call our cousin **Wofa Adu**, or Uncle Adu, because he is even older than his own paternal aunt, our late mother. Uncle Adu's father, who was the first continental or Black African to pilot a train, in 1931, was direct heir to my maternal grandfather, the Rev. T. H. Sintim, whom unfortunately the former predeceased. The elder Mr. Adu had originally trained as a teacher at Ghana's oldest and until very recently the most selective teacher-training institution, the Presbyterian Teacher-Training College at Akropong-Akwapim (or Akuapem). Uncle Adu has several grandchildren, which simply means that long before I contracted the jitters, I was already a granduncle.

In his award-winning **autobio-tirade**, titled "In My Father's House," the British-Ghanaian philosopher Kwame Anthony Appiah, a widely known fast-friend of Skip Gates', turns his nose up against his father's admonishment to uphold the family's scholastic tradition. The young Mr. Appiah, on his way to

England, his motherland, and Cambridge University, asks himself: "Just what family tradition is the old man talking about?" Unlike his *half-countryman*, both sides of this writer's family have a fairly long and respectable tradition and experience with the Western academy. For instance, the first continental African to graduate with a doctorate in Law from the University of London (1926?), Dr. J. B. Danquah, came from his agnatic family. And on his distaff side of the family, as early as the 1890s, there is a great-granduncle who was college-educated and who distinguished himself as a missionary-teacher, Nana Adu, of Akyem-Amanfrom and the Nkronso royal stoolhouse. Unlike the Asante(s), among whom Joe Appiah, or the elder Mr. Appiah, hailed, the Akyem of Ghana are well known for their litigious scholarship; they are putatively known as a people who speak from the measured or cognitive perspective of the law, even as like President George Bush II, the Asante(s) are known to speak almost wholly from the belligerent posture of raw strength or might.

11

In my search for the secret, or secrets, behind the remarkable enrollment and sterling performance of continental Africans and their African-Caribbean kin at Ivy League institutions, for the Gatesian-Guinierian Bottling Company (call it Academic Coca Cola Corporation), I came across a book written by an "indigenous" African-American titled, rather presumptuously, ***The Black Man's Guide to Working in a White Man's World*** (General Publishing Group, 1997). The name of the author is Eugene LeMay Lathan; and like Professor Gates, Mr. Lathan, a middle-level technician of a nondescript sort, gloats over the fact that he is one of a few African-Americans who live in his Vancouver, Washington, neighborhood. To this effect, the Mississippi native writes: "I live my life in the white man's world. My work and recreational lives are spent with him. I have only a couple of black friends, and they, too, live and work in the white man's world. This situation has not arisen by choice. It has happened because my job seldom deals with black businesses, nor do I live in a black-populated area./I don't know if this is good or bad. It's just the way it is. The white man's way of life is the one I grew up observing and studying. I don't wish to sound as if I'm trying to be white or that I'm telling you that the white man's way of life is the right way. The way I choose to live my life is my decision and the way you choose [to lead or live your life] is your decision./I don't expect all black men to adopt the white man's way of life, but I think it's obvious [that] we need to try something different" (***Black Man's Guide*** 93).

It goes without saying that the preceding assertion smacks of rank inferiority complex, the sort of inferiority complex that at once emasculates and deprives the subject of his very soul as a human being worthy of our respect, much less our emulation. For Mr. Lathan is fatuously disingenuous, particularly when the author asserts that his willful escape into the white community, assuming there were any such phenomenon, "has not arisen by choice." It is almost as if some white man held our dear brother at gunpoint and forced him to reside in a white neighborhood. But what makes his situation even more pathetic is the author's meticulously cultivated ambivalence, a rather ineffectual defense mechanism against his blisteringly pathological inferiority complex. And on this score, he opines: "I don't know if this is good or bad. It's just the way it is. The white man's way of life is the one I grew up observing and studying."

Needless to say, two critical problems are readily provoked by the preceding remarks. The first of these is just how a person who is ambivalent about his own choices in life comes to write a book presuming to guide another person, an African-American brother, as it were, on how to lead a successful life. The dust-jacket of Mr. Lathan's *Guide* bills the author as a diligent personage who "has worked his way through the corporate world to become a middle[-level] manager with steady employment, a loving family and a proud sense of accomplishment." And while one cannot begrudge him of his accomplishments, nonetheless, what makes Mr. Lathan assume that just about everyone of audience wants to work his proverbial butts off in order to just end up as a "middle manager [sic] with steady employment"? We have the answer; for having determined for himself that this is a bona fide white man's world, in which the rules of engagement are hermetically designed and operated by the latter, the best that he, Mr. Lathan, as an African-American could hope for is sweat his soul out and end up as a "middle manager"—a second fiddle—to a white super-ordinate or substantive manager.

We know the preceding because the very introductory paragraph of his book makes the following rather pathetically defeatist and fatalistic assertion: "The fact is, America is a white man's world, and the white man will never give up the world [that] he has worked so hard to advance. It is futile, foolish, and pitifully stupid to sit around and think [that] we are 'entitled' to something that has never been ours in the first place. Use logic. If blacks had control of life in America, would we relinquish it to someone else? No way! The reality is, no one is going to hand the good life to us. If we want to win anything, we have to play the Game" (*Black Man's Guide* 7). Indeed, what is foolish about the preceding assertion is the woeful fact that a self-proclaimed successful Black man could be thinking such patently self-emasculating thoughts. And, of course, while it is an objective reality that the proverbial white man controls America's political economy, the equally interesting fact is that, unlike Mr. Lathan, the white-American man is intelligent enough to appreciate history as a veritable wheel-of-fortune. For, rather paradoxically, having correctly observed that the proverbial white man "has worked so hard to advance" American civilization, and alongside the latter also his cause, Mr. Eugene LeMay Lathan either genuinely fails or fatuously refuses to recognize and accept the fact that no human sociopolitical situation is immutable or permanent. Then again, what makes the author assume that the African-American is innately incapable (given time and the same, or necessary, set of conditions) of applying the same purported efforts that the white man appropriated in order to take over the United States as we have come to know it?

Needless to say, one gets the sense that either the author is irreparably demented, and therefore in need of prompt and thorough psychiatric examination, or he is so morally and culturally conflicted as to crave his reader's unstinted and charitable sympathy. Or he is simply incurably ignorant. Why? Because he repeatedly, and ironically, exhorts his readers to familiarize themselves with history: "Because history repeats itself, the lessons it teaches will be valuable for your participation in the Game. You must learn the history of America and its people in order not to make the mistakes others have already made. Although your history classes may seem boring and stupid, keep in mind that someday what you are learning may help you through a problem or a rough time" (***Black Man's Guide*** 88). And here, it may be apt to ask just how did the author get into his gray-matter, as it were, that history classes "may seem boring and stupid," except if he did not take his own advice in high school? And, of course, no one says that those who have defaulted in the past could not sincerely exhort our youth to tread a more responsible path towards a more meaningful destiny. The problem is that at the time of writing his ***Black Man's Guide To Working In A White Man's World***, decades later, Mr. Lathan had still not learned anything about history. Just listen to the author jive about modern Japanese history: "It is amazing how Japan has become such a leading global power since the end of World War II. It is because they took a page from the white man's book and then developed their own system—what they considered was best suited to their way of life. What makes the Japanese people unique still exists. They are no less Japanese because of the ideas they use. If anything, they are better off, economically and culturally" (***Black Man's Guide*** 63).

Indeed, had he taken the time to learn just a little bit of Japanese history, even via the Internet, Mr. Lathan would have learned to his utter surprise and humility that on the eve of World War II, Japan ran an empire that almost rivaled that of Great Britain—and also that China and Korea, for example, were bona fide Japanese colonies. And also that as early as 1902, when the African-American descriptive or ethnic designation of "Negro" was still lower-cased by white-America, the Japanese roundly routed the Russians in a real War Game over a disputed territory. And also that the fact that most of the Asiatic countries did not undergo or experience the kind of massive socioeconomic and cultural, as well as corporeal, disruption and disorganization, disorientation and abject and outright destruction that global African people experienced during the course of the last half-millennium, has had more than a tangential impact on our collective destiny, something which the Gateses and the Guiniers of this world either fail or flatly refuse to acknowledge.

Further, author LeMay Lathan gushes: "The black race must look at the Japanese and how they adopted the changes [i.e. the purported ways of life that they borrowed from the Western white man] as a conscious effort by the entire country and its people. They started with the post-World War II generation, and trained the next generation to adapt. That generation, in turn, taught their children. Within two generations, the change has taken hold and has become the norm" (**Black Man's Guide** 63).

To be certain, as we are not wont to frankly acknowledge, the Japanese economy has far and away surpassed its imperious American counterpart. However, as already adumbrated, the process of Japanese economic, cultural and technological advancement did not exactly parallel the end of World War II (or Western War II). But more importantly, as late as 1945, African-Americans were still legally segregated and bestially penned in and herded according to the whims and caprices of the so-called American mainstream. Yet, Mr. LeMay Lathan pretends as if Black Americans were collectively slumbering or gloating over their bestial treatment by the Aryan mainstream. Needless to say, it was also during this period that Black human rights spearheads like Asa Philip Randolph, Adam Clayton Powell, Malcolm X, Martin Luther King, Jr., E. D. Nixon, Rosa Parks and Bayard Rustin, among a host of others, were poignantly about the more heroic business of both humanizing and civilizing the American white man.

12

While they lament the purported fact that the children of continental African immigrants and their Caribbean kin outnumber the children of so-called indigenous African-Americans, Professors Gates and Guinier disingenuously deny that they are pushing for the summary exclusion of the former sub-group of the global African community. And even if like Amherst College president Anthony W. Marx, one believes or agrees that the policy of Affirmative Action was emplaced primarily to serve African-Americans with predominantly American roots, there is still one question that requires a prompt and ready answer. And it is the fact that, as we have been told time and again, white women, who by any stretch of the imagination are not members of any known or recognized racial or ethnic minority group, continue to benefit more generously from Affirmative Action policies than African-Americans? And why are these African-American professors and college kingpins not making any rhetorical and political capital out of it? And we have not even begun comparing figures between continental Africans and other non-white groups, such as Hispanics and Asians who are enrolled in the concerned elite institutions of higher learning.

Interestingly but not quite surprisingly, it is a white-American liberal educator and distinguished administrator who has provided the most constructive assessment of the issue to date. Dr. Lee C. Bollinger, president of Columbia University, acutely and poignantly notes: "I don't think it should matter for purposes of admissions in higher education [whether an entrant's ancestry is continental African or Caribbean]. The issue is not origin, but social practices. It matters in American society whether you grow up black or white. It's that differential that really is the basis for affirmative action." In other words, what the former president of the University of Michigan is implicitly saying is that admissions into elite higher educational institutions must be squarely based on the kind of social equity that ensures that the best prepared candidates of all races would be accorded the optimum opportunity of developing their talents and faculties. In brief, the blind application of the proverbial ***Grandfather's Clause***, as Professors Gates and Guinier appear to be pushing, or advocating, would not wash. Indeed, if, in their own language, "indigenous" African-American students are not entering elite academic establishments as they would like to have it, such lack, as aforementioned, may squarely lie in preparation, for Affirmative Action has not been known to constitute a facile subterfuge, or excuse, for lackluster performance.

On the Caribbean-American side or front, Professors Gates and Guinier would have a hard time convincing any well-meaning or intelligent citizen, Black or White, other than themselves, that the number or percentages of the children of Caribbean immigrants enrolled at the "most selective" colleges ought to be drastically reduced or downsized in order to merely increase the intake of their so-called indigenous African-Americans. That would sound very much like an *irrational quota system*. The latter, which is largely of American mintage, pre-supposes the distribution of talent or aptitude along some curious geometric formula based on a particular group's proportional representation within the larger national populace. Going by such bizarre logic, the argument has maintained that since African-Americans constitute roughly 13-percent of America's general population, it stands to reason that every respectable or "highly selective" institution of higher learning ought to reflect this ratio or percentage of African-Americans on its roster. Consequently, it would appear that ethnic Jews, for example, are intolerably over-represented in the mainstream American media. I learned in journalism school that ethnic Jews constitute approximately 40-percent or nearly half the number of all news reporters. Conversely, among the general population, the same group is purported to constitute a mere 5-percent. Thus going by the Gatesian-Guinierian logic, there appears to be something patently unfair and even opprobrious about the preceding state of affairs. Should there have to be a drastic numerical adjustment or retrenchment, therefore, in order to ensure that professional and ideological equity or fairness prevails in the mainstream American media?

And here, the logical answer is that it all depends on one's understanding or appreciation of just what constitutes fairness or equity. Is it merely a matter of numbers or merit? This question is not that easily answerable or resolvable. For just what constitutes the criterion for measuring merit or aptitude? In all this debate, however, something quite significant is being ignored, and it is the fact of the very invention and development of the modern media. And here, also, inheres the observable question of just how and why certain groups among our human species predominate in certain fields of endeavor. It often is a simple, albeit also quite complex, set of historical circumstances. In the case of Black America, it is largely the result of systematic and perennial exclusion from the mainstream academy which has produced the unsavory climate of relative scholastic under-performance. But that this grim state of affairs is more sociopolitical than genetic or biological is attested by the fact that over the course of the last two generations, as African-Americans gained a hard-fought access into hitherto exclusive mainstream institutions, they have more than amply demonstrated their ability to readily hold their own on any proverbially level playing field.

One anonymous African-American official of a "highly selective college" is quoted by Rimer and Arenson (***New York Times*** 6/24/04) as making the following indisputably poignant observation: "If somebody does not start paying attention to those who are not able to make it in, they're going to start drifting farther and farther behind. You've got to say that the long-term blacks were either dealt a crooked hand, or something is innately wrong with them. And I simply won't accept that there is something wrong with them." But whether the best and most constructive way of paying attention to chronically underprivileged and perennially marginalized African-Americans is to disingenuously play them against diligent and tenacious continental Africans, as Professors Gates and Guinier have impudently determined to do, is another question that demands critical attention. Indeed, it cannot simply be the case that there is "something innately wrong" with the so-called indigenous African-Americans who do not appear to the likes of Amherst College president Anthony W. Marx and Professors Gates and Guinier to be performing at the expected standards. As we hinted earlier, when all is said and done, the apparently bleak performance of African-Americans in "the most selective" institutions of higher learning, vis-à-vis their continental African and Caribbean counterparts, may be more a matter of sociopolitical conditioning than anything else. The answer is partly supplied by Dr. Mary C. Waters, chairperson of the department of sociology at Harvard University. The latter, who is regarded as a leading expert on Caribbean immigrants, is quoted by Rimer and Arenson as observing that Caribbean immigrants tend to be "initially more successful than many African-Americans for a number of reasons. Since they come from majority-black countries, they are less psychologically handicapped by the stigma of race. In addition, many arrive [in the United States] with higher levels of education and professional experience. And at first, they encounter less discrimination" (***New York Times*** 6/24/04).

If Professors Gates and Guinier had bothered to talk to Professor Waters, they most probably would have also learned that after the first generation has passed on, Caribbean-Americans tend to encounter the same problems that these critics claim to be the especial preserve of "indigenous" African-Americans. Indeed, this writer earlier on gave the disturbing example of his eldest niece who, having socialized with African-Americans and been faced with the delirious nightmare of anti-African racism by the American mainstream, promptly determined that all that is culturally and intellectually empowering is white, whereas all that is sociopolitically emasculating, such as dressing up in bandanas, like a gangster, or gang-stress, and speaking in double-negatives is authentically Black. And so the question becomes not just how to ensure that chronically impoverished African-Americans gain unfettered access into "the most selective" institutions of higher education at the expense of their continental African and Caribbean kin but rather, how to effectively ensure that the second and third generations of these recent immigrants do not meet with the same fate as their so-called indigenous African-American kin. Indeed, addressing and redressing this global African dilemma requires selfless and altruistic leadership. Gauging by their rather divisive pronouncements, it hardly appears that Professors Gates and Guinier are ready to shoulder their legitimate portion of this task. In the case of Skip Gates, his "Wonders of the African World," both the television series and the accompanying book, gave the lie away.

13

The curious attempt by Harvard University professors Henry Louis Gates, Jr., and Lani Guinier to historiographically differentiate African-Americans from their African-Caribbean kin flies in the face of both common sense and historical realities. First of all, statutorily speaking, there was no recognized cultural or ethnic group by the name of African-American prior to 1868, when the United States Congress enacted some three constitutional amendments granting citizenship and the franchise to American male inhabitants of African descent. Of course, in those days, the racial and ethnic descriptive or label for the so-called indigenous African-Americans was ***Negro***, a term which almost exclusively denoted a stereotypical African, or ***Black-African***, a terminological contradiction akin to saying ***White-European***. For both "African" and "European" presuppose definitive physical types which are almost inextricably associated with "blackness" and "whiteness," respectively.

Interestingly, the geopolitical concept of "Black Africa" assumed linguistic currency sometime in the nineteenth century, or thereabouts, when it became necessary for Western European imperialists to cannibalize those parts of Africa which the latter associated with ancient advanced civilizations, ones which preceded any that were then known in the Aryan West. These parts were largely in the northern half of the African continent which, by the period under discussion, were heavily Arabized and partially Europeanized. Of course, those of us ardent students of Cheikh Anta Diop and Chancellor Williams, among a host of other African and Africanist scholars, know all too well that the northern parts of the primal continent were not the first to become civilized; neither were they always Arabized or Aryanized. That was a process that began to take remarkable shape only during the last three millennia, and three-thousand years in African history is hardly more than a proverbial drop in the bucket.

Interestingly, but hardly surprisingly, in his widely discredited television series titled ***Wonders of the African World***, Professor Henry Louis Gates, Jr., depicted an Egyptian world that hardly contained any stereotypical Africans, the so-called Black Africans. At the very beginning of the segment that dealt with Egypt, the Keyser, West Virginian native panned his camera onto a white species of humanity that looked paler than the palest of European humanity and gloated rather peevishly that this was the closest human being in Egypt that resembled the proverbial Black African. Needless to say, those Africanist scholars and students who have visited Egypt for any considerable duration and have had the opportunity to interact with the people on the ground, as it were, eloquently and confidently report that at least sixty-percent of Egyptians could not be seriously classified by any geneticist worth his or her functional designation as other than African. And yet, here we were in Mr. Gates' *Wonders of the African World* being intellectually hoodwinked and insulted.

Indeed, the peremptory significance of the year 1868 can hardly be gainsaid. Not only was it the year in which the greatest African-American thinker was born, but it was also the period during which the continental African inhabitant of these United States of America was legislatively reconstructed, long before the technology of plastic surgery was invented. This period spanning 1865 to 1877, depending on which historian one decides to cite, was called the Reconstruction Era. But it is quite moot whether any authentic reconstruction of the African personality actually occurred. For the statutory or legal identity of the latter was simply sublimated from the bizarre status of a virtual nonentity to the lurid status of second-class citizenship, if, indeed, there ever existed any citizen who was second-class at the same time. For, needless to say, you are either a bona fide citizen of a clearly defined polity or a patent slave. What is more, by 1868, this writer's maternal great-grandfather, Theodore Adolph Kwadwo Aboagye, a pioneer in the advent and propagation of Presbyterianism and Western education in the Akyem-Abuakwa State of Ghana, was a little over ten years of age. And so it is rather fatuous and ahistorical for anyone to date the history of African-Americans from 1868, as Professor Gates inadvertently appears to do. For once one buys into such ahistorical reality or perspective, the massive contributions of this branch of the continental African family to modern American civilization are summarily obliterated. For the literature produced by the likes of Olaudah Equiano (Gustavus Vassa) and Phillis Wheatley, as also by Ottobah Cugoano, for example, cannot be reckoned as *African-American Literature*. For both Phillis Wheatley and Olaudah Equiano never envisaged or identified themselves as other than African, though neither of these giants of letters was to return to the proverbial Motherland. And to be certain, Equiano was so Afrocentric that he would have readily been appalled to have been described as American or European; for his writings are full of fond memories of the African continent, particularly those of his homeland in the eastern part of post-colonial Nigeria.

The poet Phillis Wheatley, on the other hand, either because she was uprooted at the tender age of four or five years old from the Senegambia coast of West

Africa, generally exulted, paradoxically, in her unfortunate and traumatic uproot-ment, apparently because as the maid of a wealthy Bostonian family, Ms. Wheat-ley was partially shielded from the dispiriting and opprobrious brunt of chattel slavery. But she was a veritable item of chattel all the same, a second-class citizen by every definition. And she would die under harrowing circumstances. We also mentioned Dr. W. E. B. DuBois in this connection because the latter proudly acknowledged his Haitian-African roots or ancestry. And so going by Professor Gates' definition of "indigenous" African-American vis-à-vis immigrant Blacks, Black America's first scholar to graduate from Harvard University with a doctoral degree in 1896, the very year in which this writer's maternal grandfather was born, indeed, was no "indigenous" African-American, after all. In fine, Dr. Will-iam Edward Burghardt DuBois was a bona fide African-Caribbean with a squirt of French Huguenot blood; and to be certain, Dr. DuBois was so proud not to be reckoned among the White Anglo-Saxon Protestants (or WASPs) that Skip Gates would be deliriously disappointed not to be able to share his much-vaunted Anglo-Irish ancestry with Dr. DuBois. On this score, it is also quite ironic that Gates should be occupying Dr. DuBois' chair in the African-American Studies Department at Harvard University and be, actually, feeling comfortable in it! Perhaps it is about time that Skip Gates handed over his praetor's chair at Har-vard to the rightful heirs of Dr. DuBois, the children of African-Caribbean immi-grants! And so now who belongs more to the African-American Studies Department at Harvard University, but the children of continental Africans and African-Caribbean immigrants?

I have not been unfortunate enough to have become a student of Professor Gates', and it would be quite interesting to learn such from one who has had such great misfortune. For how would Skip Gates begin a lecture on African-American leadership without dealing with the sterling likes of Marcus Garvey, the father of twentieth century Back-to-Africa movement? And Percy Sutton, the pioneering president of the Borough of Manhattan? And Drs. Powell and Savoy, longtime proprietors of *The New York Amsterdam News*, arguably, until very recently the most important Black weekly of record on the East Coast of the United States? It would also be quite interesting to learn just how Skip Gates characterizes immor-talized human rights spearhead Malcolm X and Minister Louis Farrakhan, of Nation of Islam fame; Asa Philip Randolph, chief-architect of the 1963 March on Washington and master-brain of the Brotherhood of Sleeping Car Porters; what of the Rev. Adam Clayton Powell? It is not certain whether Skip Gates would also be honest enough to mention the fact that long before the majestic emergence of Barbara Jordan, Eddie Bernice Johnson, Barbara Lee and the indomitable Cynthia McKinney, there was the unquenchable Shirely Chisolm. And quite recently, there have been countless phalanges of African-Caribbean congressional representatives. And God willing, not very long from today (8/12/04), Barack Obama, the brilliant son of an East African immigrant and a white-American woman would be representing the Windy State of Illinois in the United States Senate. And here, it is also quite amusing, if not outright hilarious, to see abortive "indigenous" African-American politician Dr. Alan Keyes jump into the fray, imperiously and almost out of nowhere, claiming rather scandalously that: "I am doing this purely out of charity; the people of the State of Illinois have begged me [to vacate my home-state of Maryland] to come up to represent them." And, if one might legitimately know, was Dr. Keyes motivated by *ideological Gatesianism*, one which enjoins that only the grandchildren and great-grandchildren of erstwhile enslaved Africans in America qualify for any substantive political positions? Indeed, Messrs. Gates and Keyes may boast of having "Thirteen Ways of Looking at a Black Man," but we continental Africans and African-Caribbeans have "Three-Billion Ways of Looking at Colored People."

14

In recent years, a lot of cultural and behavioral guides have been written and published. Almost every one of them claims to contain the secrets of successful existence, even as they glibly deprecate their rivals in trade for either being lame or simply quack or fake. In this manner, these guide-book authors pretty much resemble many a televangelist who claims to have a hermetically special relationship with God and the latter's adopted son The Christ. For Christ could only be aptly conceived as the adopted son of the godhead, in view of the historical fact that the famous and immortalized Nazarene was widely known to be the son of Mary by Joseph, the carpenter. This reality, assuming that it has the kind of historiographical validity accorded it by the *New Testament*, also positions Joseph in an almost blasphemous status since, he also, like God, is regarded as the adopted father of The Christ, Jesus, that is. Which is why the entire concept of God as a purely human invention needs investigating. For Mary, reportedly, conceives The Christ in what is solemnly designated as an ***Immaculate Conception***, or ***Virgin Birth***, in global Christian circles. And, needless to say, the preceding is hard enough to grasp; however, what is even more philosophically bewildering is the fact, at least as we have been Biblically given to believe, that God then decided to have Mary betrothed to the considerably older Joseph as the latter's wife and then the "adulterous" couple proceeded to bring forth other children, Jesus' siblings, through ***Biological Conception.***

Of course, the preceding story is not new; hundreds of thousands of cultures and nations are replete with one variation of it or another. In Ghana, for example, the white father of a former premier was reported to have disowned his most successful child on the quite reasonable grounds that his long-time African mistress, by whom he had other children, had committed an act of infidelity in the very conception and birth of this most successful son. And today, though the former Scottish colonial functionary is largely immortalized by his rejected spawn, the father consistently and vehemently rejected the son to the very end of the former's life.

In any case, as noted earlier, what we are searching for here is the genie behind the sterling performance of continental Africans and their African-Caribbean kin, supposedly at the damnable expense of their "indigenous" African-American kin.

Almost like a house-divided-against-itself sort of dilemma. And this is neither a wholly new story, for 500 years of our global enslavement could not have ensured otherwise. Which is also another diplomatic way of observing the patent fact that Africans located in different portions of the globe, perforce, or logically, have different ways of thinking and pondering global phenomena. One such divergency or difference pertains to what might be termed as the *Quota Mentality* of many an African-American sociologist or academic. For instance, Professor Andrew A. Beveridge, a City University of New York, Queens, sociologist, whose ethnic or racial identity is not provided by Rimer and Arenson (*New York Times* 6/24/04), but who is herein presumed to be African-American, claims that "among 18- to 25-year-old blacks nationwide, about 9-percent describe themselves as of African or West Indian ancestry." And here also, there is quite a problem; for the largely geopolitical designation of "West Indian" is rather vague. For a West Indian ranges in ethnic and biological identity from full-blooded African to full-blooded East-Indian, with a plethora of genetic variations in-between. For instance, there is that sub-species of West Indian called or designated *Dogla* or *Dogra*, one that is of mixed African and East-Indian ancestry, who is not particularly welcomed by either curtain or aisle of the racial and ethnic divide. The late Trinidadian philosopher and scholar C. L. R. James wrote extensively about this subject, especially the seemingly intractable perennial strife, to speak much less of raw-boned animosity, between the African and East-Indian species of humanity. Then, of course, there is the traditional sub-specie designated as *Mulatto/Mulatress*, often a mixed breed issue between an African and the lecherous erstwhile slavo-colonial overlord or master. Prominent Caribbean leaders like Dr. Eric Williams, founding premier of the Republic of Trinidad, and the Manleys, of Jamaica, were known to have been of this sub-racial type or stock.

In the two cases discussed above, almost invariably, the African side of the family tends to be the more inclusive, maybe because of the fact that as the patriarchs and matriarchs of human civilization, Africans, more than any other type of the human species, appreciate the beneficent value of ethnic and racial diversity. Or there simply may be a unique genetic material that is found in greater quantities in Africans than in any of the other human species. Years ago, some African-American cultural nationalists decided that it was the human chemical called *Melanin*, which is known to be in greater quantities in the bodies of ethnic Africans than all the other major groups of humanity, and which is known to give the African her/his unique phenotype, which was largely responsible for the purported moral superiority of the African. These cultural nationalists used to organize regular, annual conferences on the question of *Melanin*, almost like an annual assembly or confabulation of the Ku Klux Klan. At these meetings, which this writer never even once attended, for it reeked to him of all that was desperate and pathetic, the ***Melanists*** reportedly gloated over their purported moral superiority over their former captors and current political overlords. ***Melanin*** was supposed to answer for all that was deemed to be culturally positive about the global African. Which was all well and good, when one reckoned the fact that for ages Europeans had been lying to themselves about their moral, intellectual and cultural superiority over all the other races by writing tomes upon tomes of dissertations denigrating non-European peoples and patting one another's backs with accolades and what they termed as ***genius awards***. Occasionally, a self-effacing or pathologically alienated African, regardless of recent geographical provenance, was called up and caparisoned with similar laurels.

Maybe it was in eager expectation of such laurels that prompted Mr. Eugene LeMay Lathan to pen and publish his ***Black Man's Guide to Working in a White Man's World*** (Los Angeles: General Publishing Group, 1997). The book, indeed, ought to have been more aptly titled ***The Blindman's Guide to Working in a White Man's World***. For it does absolutely nothing short of misguiding its unsuspecting readers. And it is almost certain that like a proverbial mirror-image, only author LeMay Lathan is wont to recognize himself or his aspirations by reading his own book. It could very well have been written by Ku Klux grand-wizard David Duke. For it has all the salient, stereotypical elements of Aryan supremacy, and the publisher may very well be so oriented. And as to how much Mr. Lathan was paid to pen such fatuous fluff, it is any intelligent African-American's good guess. The book is the very reverse of a 19th-Century ***slave narrative***; the genre, as we all know, was ironically titled, for almost all the narratives—written by the genius likes of Olaudah Equiano, Harriet Jacobs, Frederick Douglass, etc.—were actually ***Freedom*** or ***Liberation Narratives***. What Mr. LeMay Lathan's ***Guide***, unfortunately, ends up doing is attempt to herd Blackmen, the focus of his efforts, or target-audience, back into slavery and, at best, second-class citizenship. For instance, regarding the world-views or perspectives of Black and White youths, boys, to be precise, the author writes: "But I always thought of the differences between the two groups: how interested the white kids were in my life back home with my black friends and how uninterested my black friends were in the lives of those white kids…. I cannot remember anything said to me or about blacks that was derogatory." Here, it is rather pathetic that author LeMay Lathan is not intellectually sophisticated enough to recognize the patent fact that the white kids, being scions of the rulers and controllers of American society, had more than adequate luxury to expend on pitying the grim plight or bleak existential station of the proverbial African-American underdog. They had, indeed, been conditioned into being perfunctorily curious about a marginal existence which in time they would deftly exploit in order to enhance the creature comforts of the white world. The fact that his rare marginal access to the white world came through his grandmother, who served as a maid and washer-woman for an upper-class middle-class white family, is still lost on Mr. LeMay Lathan the fully-grown Black adult.

Earlier, in a strikingly [Shelby] Steelean vein, the author writes: "It would be the best thing for our race if the black youth of today hear from good role models [like Eugene LeMay Lathan?] that the plight of the black man is not just the fault of the white man, but mainly of his own doing." And so it is quite amusing when the author of **Black Man's Guide** protests as follows: "I dislike the accusation that I am just trying to be white. I'm a black man and I can never change the color of my skin. I just cannot bear to go on seeing things stay the same—we are destroying our own neighborhoods, our families, our very race."

Here again, like Professor Henry Louis Gates, Jr., and one also presumes Professor Lani Guinier, the former of whom Professor Ali A. Mazrui describes as incurably individualistic, Mr. LeMay Lathan appears to have spent the bulk of his years pursuing the proverbial Holy Grail, only to almost belatedly discover to his utter horror that he is all by himself in his enviable success, a patent victim of his own success, that is, and one that is nigh suicidal, as paradoxical as it may seem.

15

The question of quotas is a very sensitive issue, particularly where the grim historical reality of perennial exclusion prevails. There are two reasonable, or rational, approaches to resolving this dilemma, none of which is quite palatable. It is unpalatable because invariably it is the innocent sons and daughters of the barbarous fathers and passive and complicit mothers who end up paying the price, however piddling or puny. For the culture of ethnic and racial exclusion is squarely predicated on the irrational principle of *Essentialism*, the unscientific and outright callow notion that there is something fundamentally amiss with the societally constructed identity of the discursive or proverbial "Other," without the latter having been fairly accorded the fundamental opportunity to compete. And so in essence, exclusion or racial segregation presumes the abject cowardice or pusillanimity of the transgressor; for it is, ironic as it may seem, a preemptive admission of the aggressor's incompetence, which is simply reversed to make the psychologically inferior feel a grossly mistaken sense of superiority. For if one, that is the aggressor, were that confident of his or her unbested worth, then why summarily exclude potential competitors?

Indeed, the validity of the preceding observation has been more than amply vindicated in the statutory, or official, wake of racial desegregation right here in the United States. And it is further reinforced by the fact that this otherwise salutary process was never quite brought to its logical conclusion, which is why even four decades after his corporeal demise, Dr. Martin Luther King, Jr's call for the objective assaying of one's social worth in terms of diligence, or the sheer lack thereof, rather than ethnic or racial phenotype, continues to be widely quoted and cited to emphasize the fact that nearly two generations after the physical demise of the chief-architect of the Civil Rights Movement, America very much remains a product in process or, even more aptly, a tragically unfinished concept. It is almost as if the ideological concept of America as a melting-pot never quite left the proverbial drawing board.

Many of his staunch supporters and ardent critics alike are not wont to take kindly to any attempt to cast Professor Henry Louis Gates, Jr., as a "white wannabe." It is very likely to be termed as too cheap a shot to be reckoned seriously. For, needless to say, the man lives materially far more comfortably than most

Americans, Black or White, could ever fathom or dream about. And so he has acquired both the leisure and luxury of creating red herrings for those of us struggling heroically to keep our heads above the proverbial waters. And it is not simply because we are any less diligent or inventive, it is just that in the kind of impudently Darwinian environment in which Nature (or Divine Providence) sees it meed to program our destiny, the brutal collaborative scheming of the cynical and pathologically self-alienated has become the essence of good fortune, or sheer luck, and success. And here, also, it would be rather too facile and disingenuous to impute the phenomenal achievements of a Henry Louis Gates, Jr., to the purely capricious act of luck or chance. Even so, and quite intriguingly, Professor Ali A. Mazrui, of Kenya, appears to firmly believe that whatever passes for Gatesian scholarship is largely the footwork of the irredeemably self-alienated. In an essay titled "Black Orientalism? Further Reflections on 'Wonders of the African World,'" the foremost Kenyan and leading continental African political scientist, novelist and historian writes: "In fairness to Skip Gates, he himself [like Mazrui on his classic documentary titled *The Africans: A Triple Heritage*, 1986] may be receiving more positive responses from an entirely different constituency. I have no doubt [that] there is a significant market for **WONDERS OF THE AFRICAN WORLD** [upper-case lettering appears in the original], but probably not at many African Studies Centers [sic] in major U.S. universities. Africanist scholars seem to be overwhelmingly critical."

There are two issues raised here, one of which is likely to raise eyebrows in the white-American community, on whose magnanimity Skip Gates appears to have feasted or binged more than any other equally renowned *Afropean*. First is the curious notion that after all the hoopla or deafening fanfare which greeted Skip Gates during most of the 1980s in the so-called mainstream of American society, in the measured estimation of Professor Mazrui, the distinguished Albert Schweitzer chair holder at the State University of New York, Binghamton, Professor Henry Louis Gates, Jr., may, after all, not be a scholar at all. And here, also, it is significant to point out that ever the diplomatic and astute critic, Professor Mazrui is modest enough to qualify his assertion in terms of his disciplinary suasion. Thus, instead of coming out dead-on to charge Young Skippy with abject intellectual pretense or dishonesty, Professor Mazrui simply elects some of his arch-nemesis' own peers to do the job, thus the seemingly dispassionate but unmistakably caustic observation to the blistering effect that: "Africanist scholars seem to be overwhelmingly critical" (*West African Review* [2000] ISSN: 1525-4488).

The preceding is further boosted by the elderly Kenyan statesman's observation that Skip Gates' "Wonders of the African World" is likely to garner a lot of financial support in the same manner that, say, such Hollywood blockbusters as Will Smith's "I-Robot" and "Enemy of the State" did. And this is perhaps the deadliest blow that any scholar could unleash on another. And Professor Ali Mazrui, though considerably less famous than his younger White-America's poster-boy of what the latter deems to be sound Africanist scholarship, is no ordinary scholar; and he minces no words in pointing out to West Virginia's Skippy that he, Professor Mazrui, is an elder scholar. In other words, Gates is the latter's academic nephew, for Mazrui appears to envisage Gates as being hopelessly wet behind the ears, as it were, and as such Skippy ought to have first learned to crawl and ingest more organic matter before pretending or presuming to walk and rub shoulders with his intellectual superiors whom the Harvard diasporic Africanist erroneously deems as his peers. In the end, while his rejoinder contains a lot of ideas worthy of the reader's consideration, if only because it provides a credible psychoanalytical context in which to assess the scholastic validity of Gatesianism, it also verges on the dangerously personal. For instance, the concluding paragraph of Professor Mazrui's essay makes the following observation: "Some of my friends think that because I did a television series of my own, I should [or ought to] have remained silent on the series by Skip Gates. But [the immutable fact is that] I was an African long before I did a television series for the BBC and the PBS. I am responding to Skip Gates' TV series first and foremost as an African. But secondarily, I am responding to it as a senior and elder Africanist. Skip is a friend [Ha! Ha! Ha!]. But he knows [that] he and I have huge differences. If he feels [that] he has a right to criticize Africa and abuse the Swahili people and still love Africa, I feel that I have a right to criticize Skip Gates and still count him as a friend!!!" And, needless to say, all this while we thought the Bushes and Bin-Ladens were the bitterest of enemies ever.

16

The kind of dastardly attempt being engineered by Professors Henry Louis Gates, Jr., and Lani Guinier at Harvard University, in the twain's attempt to facilitate the drastic reduction in the number of continental Africans and their African-Caribbean kin at that White-American flagship institution, as well as, in their own words, the number of "non-indigenous" African-Americans at "the most selective colleges and universities," recalls a dispiriting experience that the late Pennsylvania Supreme Court justice Leon Higginbotham recounted in his legal classic titled *In The Matter of Color.* Interestingly, the latter tome was brought to my attention by my late African-Caribbean professor of African-American Studies, Mr. Edward Scobie. A very brilliant scholar, the former British Broad-casting Corporation (BBC) reporter and World War II airforce pilot, is the author of a book titled *Black Britannia*, a seminal polemic which details the often hidden "Afrocentric" lives of the British aristocracy. In the latter book, for instance, we learn, with wicked delight, that the so-called Dark Sonnets written by the immortalized William Shakespeare, were actually written as tributes to a continental African woman resident in the England of the sixteenth and seven-teenth centuries for whom the celebrated Bard-of-Avon harbored what might aptly be termed as "unquenchable affection."

The book titled *In the Matter of Color* would also be taught to me by another African-Caribbean professor, Mr. Edward Culvert, a Protestant cleric and criminological sociologist, in a course titled "Racism and the American Legal System: The African-American Experience." I mention these two professors in particular, for there were several others, in order to highlight the nigh-indispens-able impact that African-Caribbean professors have had on my education here in the United States as a student and scholar of African-American history and cul-ture.

Then, of course, there was also Professor Max Manigat, a rather urbane and dignified lawyer and an astute scholar of Caribbean history and jurisprudence. But what fascinated me more than any other thing about Professor Manigat, whose first-cousin briefly served as Haitian president during the late 1980s, was the fact that he had been a pioneering educator in post-colonial Congo-Zaire (now the so-called Democratic Republic of Congo). Shortly after Belgium handed over the reins of governance to Prime Minister Patrice Lumumba, the desperate call went out for the recruitment of teachers, for the Belgian government, the erstwhile colonial power, had done next to nothing to develop a modern cultural infrastructure for the Congo, at once Africa's richest country and its most impoverished. Professor Manigat had spent about three years in the first African country to be thoroughly colonized and Westernized helping to raise a new breed of leaders. And so in quite a significant sense, Max Manigat was a civilized man, for he had a well-informed and empirical knowledge of the African continent.

Then there was Professor Eugenia Bain, at one time this writer's favorite teacher, largely because of her ample endowment of what Jewish social scientists call ***chutzpah.*** Unfortunately, by the time that this writer left City College in 1990, Sister Bain, as she was affectionately called by the members of the African-American community, had become quite bitter, for inexplicable reasons, at continental Africans. Her parents were originally from the island of Barbados. And it appears that much of her bitterness stemmed from harrowing experiences that she had encountered as an undergraduate student at Hunter College of the City University of New York.

Sister Bain was jet-black in looks and firmly believed that the Hunter College of the 1950s, a predominantly White-American institution, had not forgiven her for her immutably Africoid, or Negroid, racial phenotype. For instance, Professor Bain recounted more than several times during class lectures, how she and another African-American classmate, the scholar Donna Richards (aka Donna Marimba Ani), had attempted to enlist into a college sorority; Sister Bain had been promptly and flatly rejected, while her bosom friend, Donna, who was light-complexioned, had been readily admitted. Indeed, whenever she recounted this patently tragic experience, it was not quite clear whether Sister Bain was actually more angry at the fact that she had been rejected by the predominantly White sorority, or the apparently grim fact that her friend Donna had unreservedly accepted the invitation to join the odious and racist sorority, or both—for Sister Bain never made it quite clear whether Donna Richards actually deserted her to hobnob with the White girls.

Interestingly enough, this writer serendipitously met Dr. Donna Richards (aka Marimba Ani) several years ago, on a queue in the HSBC bank building on Amsterdam Avenue at 96th Street in Manhattan (New York, New York). What brought them into a chance conversation was the irresistibly Afrocentric manner in which Dr. Ani was coifed. Her dread-locks reached almost to her waist-line. Earlier on, this writer had read her finely written pan-African cultural primer, ***Let***

The Circle Be Unbroken, which appears to have been later expended into a dissertation, and was promptly captivated. She was also known to hang around the culturally edifying environs of the Schomburg Library in Harlem, needless to say, an obviously natural hangout for such a brilliant scholar. Another brilliant scholar that I am itching to meet is the celebrated author of ***The Isis Papers***, a psychiatrist par-excellence, Dr. Frances Cress Welsing.

The Sister Bain story is quite interesting and worthwhile because there was far more to her mercurial temperament than the bitterness alluded to above. She was passionately Afrocentric in a way that could not be honestly said of the majority of the faculty of City College's African-American Studies department, particularly the most vociferous ones who became virtual television talk-show fixtures and screaming AWOLS of their own classrooms.

There is, for instance, the at once pathetic and repugnant case of a putative giant of City College's African-American Studies Department who rarely showed up for classes and, instead, had a barely articulate and coherent sophomore teach his ***Introduction to Black Studies*** and ***The African-American Experience*** classes for him, as an unpaid substitute. It is also rather curious, though hardly surprising, that Dr. Metooism (of course, that is not his real name) never missed collecting his paychecks at the City College's Bursar's. Sometimes this writer, who erroneously considered Dr. Metooism as an avuncular figure, personally accompanied the latter to the bursar's to collect his paycheck. But the preceding is neither the drift nor focus of the story; it is just that the inordinate rampancy of treachery makes it quite difficult for the globally Afrocentric young continental African to strike up a mentor-mentee (or protégé) relationship with many an average African-American professor, particularly a male professor. I even vividly remember defending Professor Metooism—he actually preferred the more academic title of ***Doctor*** Metooism—against a gang of some young Jewish students at City College who craved being proffered Dr. Metooidm's regal African head on the proverbial silver platter, and it may never be known just exactly how this daunting undertaking affected my fortunes. Nonetheless, I am unabashedly proud to have risen up to the occasion when even almost none of the "indigenous" African-American students would defend their, admittedly, great champion, and not a single Black City College professor would write a one-paragraph article to a newspaper in defense of their dangerously besieged colleague. To be certain, some of Dr. Metooism's own Black colleagues actually sided with the "Jerusalem Boys" in desiring the handsome noggin of their countryman on a golden platter! Among the latter were some who recalled how Dr. Metooism had rounded them up, shortly after assuming chairmanship of City College's African-

American Studies Department, like some twerps or intellectual toddlers and exhorted them callously to fend for themselves. One of the besieged New Jersey "indigene's" colleagues even recalled Dr. Metooism gloating over the fact that he possessed a doctorate—what he routinely characterized as "My Million-Dollar Education"—and ordering each and everyone of their colleagues to get one or have themselves to blame in the offing. And, quite intriguingly, Dr. Metooism's ultimatum appears to have garnered the desired effect, for as I write, the plaintiff, Professor Pangloss (not his real name, of course) today sports a doctoral degree in Sinology or Chinese Linguistics from Fordham University and is also head of perhaps the most well-respected African-American Studies department in the United States. Dr. Metooism, on the other hand, obtained his hard-earned (we shall explain this later on) doctorate from Columbia University, right here in New York City.

We point out the preceding in order to highlight the fact that the so-called indigenous African-American community is not as cohesive, both ideologically and culturally, as Harvard University's anti-continental African censors, or commissars, Professors Henry Louis Gates, Jr., and Lani Guinier would have the rest of the world believe. To be certain, Dr. Metooism even once called Professor Gates a "white loin-craving charlatan"—and here, we hasten to add that the original quotation has been remarkably doctored in order to meet the refined tastes of our audience. We also recall Justice Leon Higginbotham's legal classic *In The Matter of Color* in order to emphasize the fact that, by and large, human beings, regardless of race or ethnicity, are fundamentally divisive and nihilistic, collectively speaking, that is. For the Leon Higginbotham story is about the latter being summarily denied student lodging at the University of Pennsylvania in 1944, simply because the future judicial giant was an American of continental African descent. Exactly 60 years later, Professors Henry Louis Gates, Jr., and Lani Guinier, playing White, that is, the racist white conservative role of the dean of the University of Pennsylvania in 1944, have determined that the most suitable place of the continental African in these United States of America is exactly where mainstream society consigned Justice Leon Higginbotham back then! And we thought, rather erroneously, it turns out, that the bane of Black America was White-American racism.

It is also significant and interesting to recall that Justice Leon Higginbotham spent the final years of his life as a senior law professor at Harvard University, where his wife was also known to teach. And just what would Justice Higginbotham have said, in riposte, to such Gatesian anti-Africanism?

17

In our last installment in this series, I dissertated on my beloved professor, Jacob Metooism, largely in order to highlight the fact that the curious kind of unprovoked academic antagonism kindled by Professors Gates and Guinier at Harvard University is hardly peculiar or restricted to these so-called highly selective institutions. And maybe we need not be too quick in characterizing the Gatesian-Guinierian anti-Africanism as patently or largely "unprovoked," because when all is said and done it is, indeed, about the unanticipated success stories, or narratives, of the children of continental African immigrants, as well as their African-Caribbean kin, that are under such serious attack.

And so in a sense, Africans and African-Caribbeans, like the Jews of Nazi-Germany, during the 1930s and '40s, are being made victims of our own success stories. One would have hoped that such success stories would be seen as an empirical or scientific challenge to the putative stereotype, largely within the White-American community, regarding the purportedly innate inferiority of African-Americans, what Mr. Gates and Ms. Guinier prefer to ideologically characterize as "indigenous" African-Americans. Unfortunately, it appears as if these mordant critics of continental Africans and their Caribbean kin have pre-determined that there must, or might, be some truth or validity, however bizarre this may appear to those of us Afrocentrists who would brook no such balderdash, that, indeed, the so-called indigenous African-American is, after all, patently inferior to his or her Aryan counterpart. On this score, the Gatesian-Guinierian logic may not be radically different from the self-defeatist fatalism of Mr. Eugene LeMay Lathan, author of the so-called **Black Man's Guide To Working In A White Man's World,** the vast academic and experiential difference between these pro-Aryan players notwithstanding. For otherwise, Professors Gates and Guinier would have unreservedly decried the woeful fact that only 8-percent of Harvard University's freshmen (and freshwomen, for that matter) admitted last year were of African descent. And here also, we note the fact that the latter is measured against the established and widely accepted fact that African-Americans constitute at least 12-percent of the country's population. The natural and most rational reaction would have been for these quota-minded educators to have called for a conference with Harvard's admissions officials in order to figure out ways and means of ensuring that "indigenous" African-Americans, particularly those from economic and political underclass backgrounds, would be accorded favorable accessibility to these so-called highly selective academies. As it stands, what Mr. Gates and Ms. Guinier appear to be agitating for might be aptly termed as "intraracial reversion," or reverse-[internal-]racism, on the crassly and patently gratuitous grounds of merit, vis-à-vis continental Africans and African-Caribbean students who have proven beyond reasonable doubt their capability or preparedness to undertake, or pursue, the sort of rigorous curricular burden purported to prevail at these institutions. In fine, it is our studied contention herein that Professors Gates and Guinier are either deliberately or unwittingly advocating "dumbness" as a criterion for admitting their so-called indigenous African-American constituents.

But, unfortunately, regarding the preceding also, there is a very big problem. For while he has garnered a wide audience or following during the course of the last decade, largely through such obliquely less ideological projects as his **Encarta Africana**, Professor Gates does not appear to possess an enviable track record as an advocate for the massive education of African-Americans. Indeed, until very recently, the Keyser, West Virginian native proudly characterized himself as "an upper-middle-class" Black intellectual who did not burden, or saddle, himself with the marginal, or fluffy, cares of inner-city and rural African-Americans. And here also, as adumbrated earlier on in this series, Professor Gates made the preceding assertion as a keynoter during the 1989 Langston Hughes Festival at the City College of New York, a well-attended event in which this writer participated as an undergraduate student. And on this score, it may be worthwhile pointing out that the chief-architect, or founder, of the Langston Hughes Festival, the late Professor Raymond R. Patterson, was the creative writing teacher and mentor of this writer. On the occasion in question, however, it was another one of his African-American—actually African-Caribbean—professors, Dr. James deJongh, himself a Yale University graduate of the 1960s, who encouraged this writer and his classmates to attend. And if memory serves us right, it may also be recalled that this writer, then a graduating senior, was enrolled in one of Dr. DeJongh's courses titled "College Composition and Critical Thinking." Indeed, so fascinated has Dr. DeJongh been with Gatesian scholarship that the latter actually called his younger Harvard colleague "an institution." But here also, it goes without saying that a sizable percentage of experts in his discipline—of African-American Studies—does not concur with the notion of Professor Gates as a vintage representative of global Black scholarship, or even an institution, for that matter. For instance, in his widely cited controversial essay titled "Black Orientalism?:

Further Reflections on 'Wonders of the African World,'" Kenyan political scientist and historian Professor Ali A. Mazrui writes: "Where does RACE fit into BLACK ORIENTALISM? We must not drift into the fallacy of regarding Skip Gates' point of view as THE AFRICAN-AMERICAN PERSPECTIVE. Skip himself is such an individualist that he would be horrified by such conclusion. Even more horrified would be African-American Pan-Africanists and Afrocentrists. Almost none of them regard Gates' voice as their voice. On the contrary, Skip has denounced them in the columns of THE NEW YORK TIMES deliberately against the pictorial background of the Star of David, (God knows why!). I have talked to some very angry anti-Gates African-Americans recently. His attack on African-American nationalists and Pan-Africanists was later widely publicized and circulated by a Jewish organization" (see *West African Review* [2000] ISSN: 1525-4488).

Regarding the sticky question of Professor Gates' purportedly brazen collaboration with Jews against the collective interests of global Africans, we prefer to defer this subject to better-qualified scholars and critics. Suffice it, however, to acknowledge that Professor Mazrui's decision to introduce a Gatesian conspiracy with Jews in his rejoinder may not be purely accidental; for the leading Kenyan scholar and political scientist is an African Muslim whose ideological suasion is quite evident in much of his extensive writings. In the cited essay, for instance, Dr. Mazrui, quite understandably, questions why Professor Gates would enter the African continent, the subject of his filmic documentary "Wonders of the African World," through Tel-Aviv or Jerusalem, rather than, say, Dar-es-Salam or Dakar. And what is even more rankling to Professor Mazrui is the fact that Mr. Gates would unfavorably juxtapose the State of Israel with the Republic of Tanzania, for instance, as respective metaphorical representations of economic paradise and abject squalor. These are, needless to say, perfectly legitimate concerns. And here also, one might significantly add that Professor Mazrui has more than a tangential relationship with the Arabo-Islamic world. He proudly boasts in his extensive writings of the fact that the Mazrui family has patriarchs who emigrated from the Persian Gulf sometime during the seventeenth or eighteenth centuries, or perhaps a little later, and dominated the complex politics of the Swahili coast, after having deftly dispatched the Dutch or Portuguese "intruders" who occupied Kenya's Fort Jesus. We are not told much about the distaff side of the Mazrui family, who are reported to be indigenous African, either because much less is known about their African past worthy of an academic dissertation, or it is simply that his unabashedly Islamic orientation, a patriarchal orientation, to be certain, genuinely prevents such a potentially interesting examination.

One thing, however, has been quite troubling to this writer for some time now, and it is the fact that much of East Africa's historiography is woefully short on the coverage of non-Swahili and non-Arabo-African people. This sorry state of affairs may, indeed, very much undergird the fiercely running controversy between Professors Mazrui and Soyinka. In his filmic survey of the continent, expansively titled "The Africans: A Triple Heritage," his most ardent critics, including Professor Soyinka, Africa's pioneering Nobel Literature Prize Laureate, accuse Professor Mazrui of inordinately spotlighting the perennial conflict between Islam and Westernism almost to the total exclusion of indigenous African cultures and civilization. And when depicted, the latter is purported to be so tangential as to be deemed almost irrelevant. On the preceding score also, we prefer to defer judgment to the more experienced Africanists. It is, however, quite refreshing that Professor Mazrui in his rejoinder to Dr. Gates finally, publicly acknowledges the sources of his concept of *"The Triple Heritage"* of the modern, or post-colonial, African personality. To this effect, the highly respected Africanist scholar writes: "Although the phrase 'triple heritage' [as appropriated in Mazrui's *The Africans: A Triple Heritage*. Boston: Little, Brown, 1986] is mine, the interpretation of Africa as a confluence of three cultures was partly Kwame Nkrumah's. It was Kwame Nkrumah, founder President of Ghana, who saw Africa as an interplay of indigenous culture[s], ISLAM [sic] and what Nkrumah called Euro-Christian civilization. Before Nkrumah, Edward [Wilmot] Blyden in the nineteenth century had published his book CHRISTIANITY, ISLAM AND THE NEGRO RACE. My TV series was [thus] standing on the shoulders of those Pan African giants."

Of course, it is never too late to acknowledge one's elders, thus the global Akan symbol of *Sankofa*. We also herein acknowledge the fact that Professor Mazrui was not always the ardent and nigh-intransigent Pan-Africanist that he projects of himself today. Like Professor Henry Louis Gates, Jr., the foremost Kenyan political scientist spent most of his youth assailing the pan-Africanist agenda of Dr. Nkrumah, at one point even scornfully characterizing it as a veritable pipe-dream. And so it may, indeed, be this embarrassing phase of his career which Dr. Mazrui eerily and luridly sees reflected in the apparent academic opportunism of Professor Henry Louis Gates, Jr. And it is no great or abominable matter, for don't we all, after all, grow up sometime between our cradles and our graves?

18

The Gatesian-Guinierian game of continental African exclusion from the glorious portals of the Ivy League academies is one that I am relishing with all the utmost contempt and amusement that it squarely deserves. But it is also interesting to highlight the fact that this lurid game has been going on for quite a number of decades now. Indeed, it is akin to the kind of lethal tribal games which a horrified world witnessed during the 1990s in Bosnia, Serbia, Croatia, Rwanda-Burundi and the so-called Democratic Republic of the Congo. I have a thing or two for such histrionic appellations like "Republic" and "Democratic"; for oftentimes the designation reflects more of the aspiration than the reality. For we all know that there is nothing Republican nor Democratic about the erstwhile Central African country of Zaire. Such a conceptual mockery—or is it a parody?—is, indeed, an integral part of the colonial legacy. For as the astute Kenyan political scientist and historian Professor Ali A. Mazrui intimated in his filmic historiography of the continent, Africa remains very much a fluxional and transitional geopolitical milieu—for it is no longer an agglomeration of organic or traditional societies, for the brutal and rapid cannibalization of the continent by Western Europe ensured that this would not be the case. And neither do most of the geopolitical enclaves of the continent, with the possible exception of post-apartheid South Africa, qualify to be aptly classified as modern states.

A little learning is a dangerous thing, the celebrated and immortalized Ghanaian legal scholar and statesman Mr. Kobina Sekyi was to remind his countrymen and women at the turn of the twentieth century, with his deft crafting of a play titled **The Blinkards**. The latter was not to be published for more than a half-century after its execution. In much of his writings and pronouncements regarding the destiny of the then-Gold Coast, Barrister Kobina Sekyi prophetically noted that the effective resolution of the damaging effects ensuing in the wake of Africa's encounter with Europe between the fourteenth and the turn of the twentieth centuries was bound to largely determine the former's ability, or lack thereof, for that matter, to transition into an authentic state of sovereignty. On another level, the preceding may be aptly seen to have echoed Dr. W. E. B. DuBois' measured prediction in his 1903 classic **The Souls of Black Folk**, that the central dilemma of twentieth-century American politics would hinge squarely on the problem of the **color line** or **color bar**, as it became widely known in apartheid South Africa.

Back then, it is almost certain that Dr. DuBois could not have predicted the apocalyptic rage of Nazi Germany, otherwise known as the holocaust, though having studied in that great Western European nation, Dr. DuBois must have experienced subtle hints of the xenophobic German national temperament. For the Nazi holocaust was tantamount to intra-racial and tribal genocide, just like the grim instances witnessed in Liberia, Sierra Leone, Congo and Rwanda. In Liberia, the source of conflict, as Barrister Kobina Sekyi accurately predicted, was the slavo-colonial legacy. And the Liberian conniption, tragically staged between the so-called America-Liberians and their "indigenous" compatriots is, perhaps, the most relevant and interesting question worth raising in this context for, indubitably and eerily inescapably, the Gatesian-Guinierian game of political exclusion mirrors the Liberian civil war. The details of the two instances are quite pedestrian or commonplace. What needs to be both highlighted and lamented is the gross failure of the purportedly highly cultivated intellect to rise above nihilistic primal, human instincts and promptly remedy a potentially chaotic situation. In sum, it is our solemn and unctuous contention herein that by their curious and grossly unfortunate expression of hostility towards continental Africans, Professors Henry Louis Gates, Jr., and Lani Guinier have brought great shame, to speak less of outright disgrace, to bear on the otherwise inviolable dignity of their profession. And to think that these "mainstream" Black educators rank themselves among the cream of African-American professoriate, is one that needs urgent and thorough re-examination. In the Liberian instance, among the plethora of regrettable grievances leveled against the so-called America-Liberians was the purportedly deliberate attempt by the latter, who predominated the country's government in the pre-Doe era, to summarily exclude non-America-Liberians from the august portals of the country's flagship academies, as well as, in Gatesian-Guinierian parlance, being excluded from "the inner-circles of power." And this is quite interesting because it eloquently upends the Gatesian-Guinierian argument, implicitly, that somehow "the descendants of slaves" possess a kind of moral innocence that is woefully lacking in those of us who might not be able to point to a great-grandmother or great-grandfather, for that matter, who was classified as chattel here in the United States during the nineteenth century and before. For needless to say, most of the ancestors of the present-day's so-called America-Liberians are known to have been enslaved right here in the United States. In fine, it is our contention here that the disingenuous attempt by Professors Guinier and Gates to differentiate the destiny of African-Americans, the so-called indigenous ones, that is, from the destiny of continental African and Caribbean immigrants is simply chimerical. For fundamentally, there are no clear-cut villains and victims vis-à-vis the deleterious impact of the global African Holocaust. For there were Africans, on the proverbial Motherland, who lost relatives—parents, siblings and uncles and aunts—in the perennial and harrowing process of our collective enslavement, and with the latter the ineluctable concomitant of the kind of economic deprivation experienced by the Southern Black-American, whom Skip Gates and Lani Guinier prefer to euphemistically tag as "the chronically poor."

Needless to say, it is almost certain that Skip Gates' Irish family were as equally complicit in the enslavement and abject exploitation of continental Africans, as those nefarious African chiefs and their impudent associates who unconscionably collaborated in facilitating the establishment of the infamous Peculiar Institution. Or, does Professor Gates naively presume the existence of discrete sovereign and slave states on the continent, the former of which routinely preyed on the latter to facilitate the repugnant trade in African humanity? And, indeed, the proud West Virginian *racial hybrid* (Skip Gates' own self-categorization) might do himself great good to research or investigate the number of powerful and wealthy "indigenous" African-Americans who eagerly and remorselessly participated in the abject enslavement and exploitation of their own kind. It is quite certain that Skip Gates would be flabbergasted by what he discovers. And it should not be very difficult for the well-endowed Harvard humanities scholar to undertake such a project. His impudent and irreligious attempt to demonize and bestialize continental Africans is unlikely to be either forgotten or forgiven by future students of African Studies. And it is rather insulting to the global African community that Professor Gates should be allowed to occupy a chair named for Dr. W. E. B. DuBois, a Haitian-American who was neither afraid nor ashamed to renounce his United States citizenship in order to be conferred with Ghanaian citizenship by President Kwame Nkrumah.

19

I have dwelt considerably on the curious case of the celebrated Dr. Jacob Metooism, celebrated more by way of notoriety, of the City College of New York, because the dastardly scheme being engineered by Harvard University professors Henry Louis Gates, Jr., and Lani Guinier to ensure the drastic and systematic exclusion of continental Africans and their African-Caribbean kin from the august portals of the Ivy League is nothing new; and neither is it occurring only at Harvard and the other so-called most-selective colleges and universities in the United States. In 1990, for instance, when this writer was in the process of applying for graduate studies at Temple University, he approached Dr. Metooism with a recommendation form; the former felt that such a move was only natural because for a year-and-half, he had been studying the seminal historiographical works of Cheikh Anta Diop under the rather erratic supervision of Dr. Metoosim. In hindsight, this writer ought to have known that Dr. Metooism was not the best person to approach on such a pressing and crucial matter; for in spite of the latter's stentorian pronouncements about the unstinted support of his Ghanaian ancestors, throughout his hectic battles with the American-Jewish community, in particular, and the American mainstream in general, on national radio and television, as well as in such newspapers of record as *The New York Times*, the then-besieged New Jersey "indigene" did, indeed, appear to harbor remarkable suspicion of continental Africans.

And the source of such lurid suspicion appeared not to be far-fetched; several years before, the good, old Doctor Metooism had bitterly battled a Ghanaian professor by the name of Dr. Botchway who ran the Africana Studies Department prior to the histrionic arrival of Dr. Metooism, reportedly, from somewhere in the South-West. The battle in question was supposed to have been rather routine and impersonal, a terminal election or re-election of a departmental head. According to reliable sources, for some curious and capricious reasons, Dr. Metooism possessed some sort of religious, or fetishistic, sense of entitlement, merely by virtue of having been born and bred right here in the United States. And so in essence, any non-American-born African who contested the chairmanship of the Africana Studies Department at the City College of New York was promptly perceived as a dangerous intruder, or an interloper, who needed to be dispatched forthwith. In essence, that was exactly what happened to Professor Botchway. The latter, legend had it, would shortly thereafter end up somewhere in the Mid-West—the Ohio area, or some such municipality—and shortly thereafter back in Ghana, from whence he had emerged, as it were.

It is also quite significant and interesting to observe, at this juncture, that Professor Botchway was a good friend of this writer's late father's. Nonetheless, this writer's father continued to have great respect for Dr. Metooism; for the former regarded the latter as a courageous scholar in the uncompromising mold of Malcolm X. The latter's kind of bravado did not earn our subject much public approbation, not even within his own African-American community, a community that continues to be harried by the imperious and dehumanizing vagaries of capitalism; still, dignity was a coveted personality trait which no one, not even Divine Providence, could begrudge Malcolm X and, this writer's father strongly maintained, the great Dr. Jacob Metooism. The old man also found the pioneering courage possessed by the likes of Harriet Tubman, Fannie Lou Hamer, Rosa Parks and Martin Luther King, Jr., for a few remarkable instances, to be sorely lacking among the African-American intellectual leadership of the 1970s and '80s. Needless to say, the validity of the preceding assessment might be reasonably deemed moot.

Unfortunately, it appears that Dr. Metooism's putatively altruistic courage did not extend to this continental African writer. Let the reader not make the flagrant error of presuming that this writer was in dire search of woefully undeserved charity or favor. For he had, it may be significant to recall, spent more than half of his three-and-half years at City College vehemently defending Dr. Metooism against his teeming legions of detractors, both from among the formidable ranks of the professoriate as well as the City College administration. But, perhaps, even more importantly, being that he had studied under Dr. Metooism for nearly half of his stay as an undergraduate student at City College, the least that this writer expected by way of teacher-student relationship was such rather routine gesture as writing a recommendation letter for one's loyal and devoted student, such as the latter was. Interestingly enough, even on the occasion being herein recalled, it was not a tedious matter of sitting down for even a half-hour and cranking out the sort of fulsome letter-of-recommendation which no administrator worth his or her name on paper would care to read.

I know precisely what I am talking about, being a fourth-generation educator myself and also one is from time to time called upon by some of my former students to write them recommendation letters. It was a simple recommendation form that merely required a check-mark or two, and a terse sentence or two affirming the capability or preparedness of the applicant to undertake the puta-tively rigorous regime of graduate studies. And here, we report with great sadness, shame and utmost regret that rather than honestly and frankly decline my polite and solemn request for recommendation to the Temple University Graduate School of the Arts and Sciences, Dr. Metooism simply accepted my recommen-dation form with the promise of filling and mailing it to Philadelphia and promptly dumped it into his office's waste-paper basket! This writer would shortly upon gaining admission into Temple University's Department of African-American Studies pay a courtesy call on Dr. Metooism and express his profound gratitude, only to learn a short while later, through an unforeseen verbal disagree-ment with his graduate-school roommate and former classmate at City College, that the avuncular Dr. Metooism had actually sneered behind his back and made snide remarks before crumpling up his recommendation form and pitching it, basketball style, into Dr. Metooism's office's waste-paper basket.

Shortly thereafter, this writer ascertained, or rather confirmed, the veracity of Mr. Olumba Obumba's curious notification by asking his graduate school advi-sor, Dr. Abu S. Abarry, to examine his academic file to see whether his advisor could locate any recommendation form from Dr. Metooism. A few days later, this writer received an answer in the negative. The latter's reaction by now had turned from one of shock and surprise, to speak much less of outright disappoint-ment, into one of knowing amusement, for he was more ashamed than upset or even angry. After all, did not the good, old *Afropean* have every right to either help or undermine whomever he so deemed, as his conscience saw it meed to order him?

Of course, I was hurt to the quick with shame and disappointment because for most of the duration prior to being apprised of his treachery, I had been bragging about how I had been privileged to have studied with Professor Metooism. Look-ing back at the entire episode, however, I realize that it was the best experience of my life. For I realize how utterly naïve I had been in not paying heed to the semantic essence of the name of Dr. Metooism, for the essence of his character was boldly etched therein! Now his name also reminds me of that Akan maxim which exhorts that: "When Mr. Naked promises you a bolt of cloth, just be wise enough to listen to his name."

Paradoxically, this tragic episode has enhanced my respect for Dr. Metooism, for it has taught me the indispensable lesson that we are all only too human. It has also apprised me of the curious fact that even the seemingly most privileged and powerful among us could sometimes harbor great envy, and even animosity, towards the patently underprivileged nobodies, relatively speaking. But most of all, it gladdens my soul to know that contrary to my initial belief and impression, as an educator, Dr. Metooism has the least claim on my fortunes; not that I have been as fortunate as I would like to be, though reading the jaundiced remarks of the gargantuan likes of Professor Henry Louis Gates, Jr., assures me of the palpable fact that the greatest scalers-or-limbers—of Mount Everest have yet to arrive. Of course, the preceding recalls the title of a novel written by Mr. Ayi Kwei Armah, the foremost Ghanaian and African prose stylist; the novel is titled *The Beautyful Ones Are Not Yet Born*. Significantly, Mr. Armah graduated with *summa cum laude* and a Bachelor's degree in Sociology from Harvard University when Skip Gates was barely eleven or twelve years old. And in those days, before Affirmative Action fully came into the picture, there were far less numbers of "indigenous" African-Americans enrolled at Harvard than today. The polyglot Mr. Armah also obtained a Master's degree from Columbia University, right here in New York City, when Skip Gates was barely aware of the harrowing global African condition. Earlier on, the renowned Ghanaian thinker had attended the elite Groton Institute in Rhode Island, the formative intellectual wash-basin of the Kennedys, among others. And legend has it that by the mid-60s, when Mr. Armah enrolled at Columbia University to study Creative Writing, the Ghanaian novelist was more famous than almost every one of his professors. And if you were to ask of his primary motivation, it is quite certain that climbing into the inner-circles of White-American society was not even on his radar screen, as it were. For Mr. Armah would quit his plum teaching post at the University of Wisconsin, Madison, to set up abode, or pitch his proverbial tent, in a remote Senegalese village. It was simply out of plain disgust for White-America's socio-political pretensions. Unlike Skip Gates, Mr. Armah did not need to sport Harvard and Columbia T-shirts in order to remind himself of his worth in the protean scheme of human existence.

20

In his perspicuous and edifying rejoinder to Henry Louis Gates' "Wonders of the African World," Kenyan scholar, cultural historian and political scientist Ali A. Mazrui raises the grim but significant question of "internal collaborators" who either wittingly or unwittingly facilitated the damnable portrayal of continental Africans as unconscionable, pathological slavocrats. To the foregoing effect, Professor Mazrui, who is also a remarkable programmatic novelist, writes: "To my astonishment when [while?] watching 'Wonders of the African World,' I heard a Ghanaian tourist guide at a slave fort (Elmina) tell [a group of] African-American tourists that they were sold into slavery by Africans. Is this [sic] the policy of the Ghanaian government to tell tourists that it was not the white man but the Black man who was responsible for the Atlantic slave system? If not, why is not the guide sacked? He was [in effect] saying to African Americans [:] 'We Ghanaians sold you!'" ("Black Orientalism?: Further Reflections on 'Wonders of the African World.' *West African Review* [2000] ISSN 1525-4488).

Needless to say, the preceding abstract raises several troubling questions. First of all, Professor Mazrui does not indicate his awareness of the fact of whether the Ghanaian tourist guide who sophomorically asserted that Africans unreservedly, or even eagerly, participated in the massive and callous enslavement of their own kin and neighbors was still at his post at the time that the renowned scholar wrote and published his rejoinder. Consequently, his query as to whether the Ghanaian government maintained a curious policy of telling tourists that it was not the white man but the Black man who was responsible for the Atlantic slave system, sounds more insulting than surprising. This, however, is not to imply that Professor Mazrui has a low opinion of either the Ghanaian government or the Ghanaian people at large; for the distinguished director of the Global Studies Institute at the State University of New York, Binghamton, has paid several lecture tours to the country and written extensively and largely positively about the place and the role of Ghana in both continental African and global affairs. But, perhaps, even more significantly, Professor Mazrui is so highly regarded in Ghana that he is frequently called upon to offer his opinions on matters pertaining to the peace and stability of the region.

Indeed, the painfully thoughtless pronouncements of the Ghanaian tourist guide interviewed by Skip Gates during the filming of the latter's infamous "Wonders of the African World," reflected more on the woefully inadequate historiographical curriculum of many a Ghanaian educational institution, as well as the entire African continent, than any deliberate attempt either on the part of any individual or the Ghanaian government to misinform an unsuspecting American audience. Indeed, even in his celebrated textbook titled *Topics in West African History*, Professor A. Adu Boahen leaves virtually no other remarkable impression than the fact that the Asante people and their leaders willfully and happily participated in the massive and protracted enslavement of their own people. And, in fact, even at the dawn of the British abolition of African enslavement when the regnant Asante king, or Asantehene, was informed to the preceding effect, the latter is reported to have vehemently protested on the grounds that abruptly stanching the massive commercial efflux of human merchandise would drastically jeopardize the status and economic prosperity of the Asante empire. And to a remarkable extent this preceding observation contained some validity; for nearly three centuries before, the entire economy of the Asante empire had come to rely almost entirely on human traffic. It also did not effectively help matters that the British, and the other European powers involved in the slave trade, initially used moral arguments to stanch a culture or commercial regime that had been wholly predicated upon economic interests. Consequently, it was to take a strong European military presence to halt the lurid trade in African humanity. Interestingly, and rather disingenuously, it is this aspect of the Slave Trade that is often presented by Western apologists and neo-slavocrats as evidence of the limited culpability of Western Europe in the massive and protracted enslavement of African humanity. What is often omitted in the telling is also the significant fact that the overwhelming majority of the military forces employed to stanch the Slave Trade were continental Africans, as well as some African-Caribbeans largely reimported, or repatriated, by the British from such colonies as Jamaica and Barbados. About ten years ago, while this writer was teaching at the Indiana State University in Terre Haute, distinguished American History professor Arthur Schlesinger, Jr., who was also a speech-writer for President John F. Kennedy, gave a lecture in which the Harvard-educated historian presumed to effectively topple the Afrocentric school of thinkers, particularly those resident at Temple University, by making the disingenuous claim that the abolition of slavery was prompted largely by the unique ethical refinement of the Western white man. Professor Schlesinger, however, woefully failed to logically explain the fact that it took more than half-century, between 1807 and 1865, for the Western white man of the United States to proscribe the proverbial Peculiar Institution here in the United States.

To be certain, a far more balanced perspective on the complex dynamics of the slave trade has been provided by the late African-Guyanese scholar of genius Dr. Walter Rodney, in the latter's seminal classic titled *How Europe Underdeveloped Africa*. In the preceding treatise, Dr. Rodney cites a plethora of instances regarding the desperate attempts initiated by traditional African rulers in stanching the unhealthy efflux of African humanity long before any European leaders conceived of the need to stop the destructive traffic in African humanity. The extensive writings of authoritative British historian Basil Davidson are also replete with balanced perspectives on the Slave Trade. And most recently, the polymathic Nigerian scholar Dr. Chinweizu, in his well-researched and erudite monograph titled *The West and the Rest of Us*, has provided us with a more comprehensive and pragmatic view on this problematic subject. And here, also, it is significant to note that some conservative historians and political scientists, both Black and White, have dismissed the aforementioned works by Drs. Rodney and Chinweizu as amounting to nothing more than strident polemics. And it is likewise significant to also note that none of these critics have made any peremptory or proprietary claims to the facts surrounding our subject of discourse.

We also note the fact that Professor Mazrui, in his otherwise eloquent and powerful rejoinder to Professor Gates' "Wonders of the African World," appears to be either morally conflicted or, curiously enough, awed into expressing what might be deemed tantamount to fawning affection. Did such lame ratiocinative tack, or approach, have anything to do with Professor Mazrui's fear of the certain possibility of sustaining another unwelcome attack from Nigeria's Nobel Literature laureate Professor Wole Soyinka, Skip Gates' academic uncle? We pose the preceding question because regarding the historiographical misguidance of the aforementioned Ghanaian tourist guide at Elmina Castle, Professor Mazrui almost apologetically writes: "The Ghanaians [that] I have spoken to since Gates' television series are convinced that the Ghanaian guide at the slave fort was given an 'inducement' to blame the slave trade on Africans! Who is behind this rewriting of the history of the slave trade? *I am sure [that] Gates was as surprised as I was when he heard such frankness from a Ghanaian tourist-guide*" (Italics added).

In the preceding, it is not quite clear whether Professor Mazrui is being simply sarcastic, or the elderly Africanist scholar, as he prefers to call himself, is just trying to fool his readers. First of all, why would the distinguished Albert Schweitzer professor of the humanities, for instance, suggest that someone had, perhaps, "induced" the Ghanaian tourist-guide implicitly via a patently reprehensible act of bribery, in order to mislead his clients, and not divulge to his readers the likely identity of the culprit? And then, there is also a striking element of the disingenuous when Professor Mazrui states that: "I am sure [that] Gates was as surprised as I was when he heard such frankness from a Ghanaian tourist-guide." It is not quite clear where he has been all this while, or the Kenyan political scientist simply has no idea about the putative Ghanaian national temperament. For almost no group of people or nationality on the African continent is known to be as naturally forthcoming, forthright and frank as the Ghanaian. Furthermore, the critic's summary call for the Ghanaian tourist-guide to be removed, on the quite reasonable grounds of official misrepresentations, nevertheless, reeks of ideological autocracy. And this is rather pathetic, coming from a scholar who was once a political prisoner under the lackluster regime of President Daniel Arap Moi. Needless to say, Ghana is currently a constitutional democracy as well as a liberal society that tolerates epistemic and ideological diversity. In sum, the statal policy is not to summarily fire anybody just because of his or her ignorance, or even plain stupidity. Instead, what is called for is a curricular, or historiographical, re-education

21

In his celebrated and quite eloquent rejoinder to the veritable hatchet work that was Henry Louis Gates, Jr's, filmic documentary titled "Wonders of the African World," Kenya's Ali A. Mazrui raises the indubitably significant question regarding the Eurocentric, collaborative agenda of the narrator-filmmaker. To this effect, Dr. Mazrui observes: "Now Skip Gates' television series virtually tells the world that the West has no case to answer. Africans [, in effect,] sold each other. Presumably if there are to be any reparations in the trans-Atlantic slave-trade, it would have to be from Africans to African Americans. Skip Gates succeeded in getting an African to say that without the role of Africans in facilitating it, there would have been no trans-Atlantic slave trade at all."

Here again, there are a few problems requiring prompt addressing. First is what might aptly be termed as ***the negative psychology of historiographical sanitation***. And the latter alludes to the fact that in his documentary titled ***The Africans: A Triple Heritage***, particularly the textbook accompanying the latter, Professor Mazrui almost lauds the fact that continental Africans were massively deported into the so-called New World. The leading African political scientist thinks that this bizarre process, somehow, was a salutary way of ushering Africans into the dubious era of modernism. And this is a quite curiously bizarre way of envisaging matters pertaining to continental Africa's geopolitical and economic destiny over the past half-millennium. More so, when even distinguished British historian Basil Davidson has poignantly lamented the way and manner by which Western Europe brought continental Africans into the ambit of the so-called Modern World, or modernity, particularly when one reckons the massive contributions that Africans made towards the fabrication and development of Western civilization. And so, in a quite bizarre sense, just as Professor Henry Louis Gates, Jr., "succeeded in getting an African to say that without the role of Africans in facilitating it, there would have been no trans-Atlantic slave trade at all," we find Professor Mazrui applauding the grim historical circumstances that forcibly introduced Africans into the modern European world. Indeed, if memory serves us accurately, the highly respected Kenyan scholar describes the foregoing event as a "mixed blessing" where most of us Africans, as well as Africanists, simply recognize the trans-Atlantic slave trade as an unmitigable tragedy. And could this—it may be aptly surmised—have anything to do with the fact that Dr. Mazrui seems to invest much capital in the Arabo-Islamic, or the Mazrui side, of his family? For almost no African who fully appreciates the perennial humiliation and abject marginalization of the global African personality would either recognize the African Holocaust as one that entailed some protean and bizarre element called "a mixed blessing", or "salutary modernism."

We boldly and unabashedly make the preceding observation because in his mordant rejoinder to Henry Louis Gates, Jr., titled "Black Orientalism?: Further Reflections on 'Wonders of the African World,' Professor Mazrui makes a special or specific issue out of the fact that the West Virginian native could muster the effrontery to criticize "the Swahili people." And here, the latter ethnic group is cast in a virtually vacuous and near-abstract milieu of Africanity, much the same way the Joseph Conrad's imperial classic **Heart of Darkness** was caustically assailed for according short-shrift treatment to the proverbial African personality. To the preceding effect, Professor Mazrui writes furiously at length: "Some of my friends think that because I did a television series of my own, I should have remained silent on the series by Skip Gates. But I was an African long before I did a television series for the BBC and the PBS. I am responding to Skip Gates' TV series first and foremost as an African. But secondarily, I am responding to it as a senior and elder Africanist. Skip is a friend. But he knows [that] he and I have huge differences. *If he feels he has a right to criticize Africa and abuse the Swahili people and still love Africa, I feel I have a right to criticize Skip Gates and still count him as a friend*!!!"(Italics added; the treble exclamation marks, however, appear in the original).

Now, anybody who is reasonably acquainted with the English language knows that there is a remarkable difference between the infinitive verbs "to criticize" and "to abuse." To criticize, however adversely, is almost invariably and inevitably a salutary act of the critical and scholarly mind. To be certain, it would have been quite strange, even outright bizarre, had either Skip Gates or Professor Mazrui not criticized what these gentlemen believed to be the unsavory or untoward aspects of African history and culture, particularly African leadership, in their respective documentaries. On the other hand, to accuse a colleague of being "abusive" of one's history and one's ethnicity or people, is a wholly different issue altogether. In fact, the latter undoubtedly verges on the flagrant, egregious and outright criminal. In essence, here, Professor Mazrui allows what might be aptly termed as his "micro-nationalism" to impede the otherwise poignant thrust of his observations. The foregoing assertion is further boosted by the following salvo launched at Skip Gates and his supporters, under the quite useful and handy label of "Black Orientalism": "Some of you have expressed surprise that I included a reference to Jewish capital in the Trans-Atlantic slave trade. There were several reasons. Gates has sometimes used Jewish symbols in his attacks on Pan-Africanists and Afrocentrists. Secondly, Gates has used a significant part of his television series to expose ARAB participation in the slave trade. Why not complete the Semitic picture and refer to the JEWISH participation in the trade?"

Here, the mistake that Professor Mazrui makes is to foreground the entire indigenous African and Western-European debate as an Islamo-Hebraic problematic, and in the process the real and major players are relegated to the margins, and we pathetically end up with another side-show on the so-called Middle-Eastern crisis. In sum, Professor Mazrui hijacks African primacy in the discourse on the trans-Atlantic slave trade. Consequently, whether it would have been more apposite or appropriate for Skip Gates to have worn an African shirt, instead of a Jewish one, becomes totally irrelevant and almost patently absurd. And the fact that "many African Americans wear such [i.e. traditional African] shirts right here in the United States routinely," as Professor Mazrui claims, is also quite irrelevant, for Skip Gates is not "many African Americans," and even Professor Mazrui himself acknowledges earlier on in his rejoinder that Uncle Skippy is too pathologically individualistic for his scholarship, or any lack thereof, to reflect the mainstream of African-American thought or ideology. The State University of New York, Binghamton, Albert Schweitzer scholar also contradicts himself by further adding, parenthetically, that: "Gates was ceremonially dressed in [the] Sudan and in Kente regalia for a Ghanaian occasion, but he managed a few snide remarks and jokes in the process." In fact, as tragically undignified as some aspects of his Ghanaian presentation were, nevertheless, it was in Ghana that Skip Gates exuded his most charming and eloquent best. And this is not a light statement for this writer to make, in view of the Byzantine complexities regarding this subjective question.

Professor Mazrui also mentions the grim fact that "Skip Gates succeeded in getting an African to say that without the role of Africans in facilitating it, there would have been no trans-Atlantic slave trade at all." Here again, the fact that the foremost Kenyan political scientist does not mention the name of the subject of his perceived betrayal of the global African cause is quite fascinating and curious, if only because it exhibits the critic's unreserved contempt for the purported "traitor," as it were. For Dr. Akosua Perbi, the African woman who made the preceding remark, is no ordinary Ghanaian, or African, woman, for that matter. She was head or chairperson of the Department of History at the University of Ghana, Legon, during Skip Gates' filming of his "Wonders of the African

World," and her name and credentials were given on the screen as such. And while she, understandably, might not have come off to Professor Mazrui as a very impressive scholar of her discipline, nonetheless, as head of a department at Ghana's flagship academy, at least she deserved to have been courteously recognized as such. It is also significant to note that Dr. (Mrs.) Akosua Perbi is the eldest daughter and child of distinguished Ghanaian musicologist, Professor J. H. (K.) Nketia, who is also arguably the foremost living musicologist on the African continent, as well as founder of the University of Ghana's Institute of African Studies, one of the oldest and most respected of its kind on the African continent. Maybe it was his Islamic conservatism which prevented Professor Mazrui from according Dr. Perbi her basic human and professional recognition.

The preceding notwithstanding, there are several factors which prompted Dr. Perbi to respond to Dr. Henry Louis Gates, Jr., in the manner that she did during the latter's filming of his nihilistic documentary titled "Wonders of the African World," a subject which is expansively discussed in the next segment of this series.

22

To fully appreciate why a Ghanaian tourist-guide would assume unreserved and collective blame—or guilt—for the enslavement of African-Americans, and also for a Ghanaian academic to myopically—and ahistorically—maintain that without the active participation of Africans the trans-Atlantic slave trade would not have occurred, one needs to understand the proverbial, conciliatory Ghanaian temperament. Unlike many of their diasporic African kin, the Ghanaian, by nature or culture, is not very confrontational. In fact, even the Asante of Ghana who have been variously described by their enemies and adversaries, particularly the British, as belligerent, domineering and warlike, have also been recognized for their political diplomacy in the most volatile situations. The Asante are also known to be, perhaps, the most hospitable nation among continental Africans. Sometimes their mild-mannered temperament and rarefied hospitality have misled their detractors and rivals into envisaging the Asante as being cowardly, although more than ample evidence points to the virtually unbested courage of the Akan, particularly the Akyem and Asante, of the West African sub-region.

As traditional imperialists, if there were any such expression or phenomenon, the Asante, for instance, at the height of their glory exerted political influence over an area three times the size of modern Ghana. Almost no single traditional polity, with the possible exception of the Hausa states of Northern Nigeria, exerted that much impact, both in economic and political terms. And, indeed, so relatively culturally refined were the Akan that at the dawn of their encounter with the Europeans, the latter were very puzzled regarding the fact of how a pre-literate society could found, develop and maintain a constitutionally monarchical system that in many instances dwarfed its counterparts in the Europe of the Fifteenth and Sixteenth centuries. Consequently, plausible attempts have been made by historians and scholars, both African and foreign, to link contemporary Ghanaians with such celebrated ancient and medieval civilizations as Egypt and Nubia, Ghana, Mali and Songhai. Even in the textbook accompanying his television series titled *The Africans: A Triple Heritage* (1986), Professor Ali Mazrui notes the fact that the relative sartorial elegance, felicity and sophistication of West Africans, particularly the Akan of Ghana, are unparalleled—or unprecedented—in the entire continental sub-region of the so-called Black Africa. And while he sounds sarcastic in his acknowledgment of fact, the Kenyan scholar, nevertheless, also claims to be privy to a purported secret behind such sartorial sophistication, though he prefers to maintain his silence on this enviable cultural achievement. It is almost certain that what causes him not to broach the issue any further regards a possible external factor, one that is wont to be met with fierce disagreement from both students and scholars of West African history, civilization and culture.

Upon the fear of sounding nationalistic, I make bold to assert that the Ghanaian national conscience is perhaps the most acute on the entire African continent. We learn of a similar trait among the leaders of medieval Mali and, indeed, some linguisticians have assayed the plausibility of such historical and genetic affinity. And, indeed, it was not for nothing that modern Ghana's founder and premier, Dr. Kwame Nkrumah, wrote a book titled *Consciencism*, in which he poignantly discusses the collective and proactive destiny of the global African personality. In sum, on the question of the infamous trans-Atlantic slave trade, particularly the indubitable African participation in it, many reasonably well-educated Ghanaians feel an acute and searing sense of guilt that most African-Americans may almost certainly find extremely difficult to comprehend. And, to be certain, this writer has had such question directly put to him by a well-respected African-American scholar and educator. Years ago, while an undergraduate at the City College of New York, my avuncular friend and mentor Professor James Small asked of me during a sobering moment of reflection on our collective, global African destiny: "Now tell me, Kwame, why did you people sell us to the white man?" Needless to say, as I recall the preceding conversation nearly twenty years later, my eyes are suffused with tears. I experienced a similar sensation while reading novelist Alice Walker's Pulitzer Prize-winning fiction titled *Color Purple*. I wept like a child, just like that terse passage in the Bible which reports of Jesus as having broken down and wept profusely. I suppose the latter was in logical response to the reported demise of Christ's bosom friend Lazarus.

Indeed, the painful and ignominious legacy of our enslavement as a people is one that would continue to run as a sore in my heart for as long as I live; for, in the final analysis, the dehumanizing process of African enslavement was a double-edged sword that psychologically debilitated both the continental African and his or her diasporic African kin, including the African-Caribbean, as well as those of us who found our way and permanently altered destiny in the Arabo-European world. Indeed, for most Africans, particularly the highly educated and enlightened—for these two cultural categories are neither synonymous nor necessarily interchangeable—reading African history over the past half-millennium is an excruciating exercise in our collective and perennial humiliation. To be certain, only the crassly unenlightened attempt to except or differentiate themselves from the proverbial diasporic African experience. And when Columbia University president Lee C. Bollinger emphasizes the glaring fact that at the bottom: "It matters in American society whether you grow up black or white," this is unmistakably what the renowned Affirmative Action expert means—in essence, and by extension, the sociopolitical, economic and cultural marginalization of the African-descended person is global. Unfortunately, this visceral reality seems to be totally lost on the cynical and callow likes of Professors Gates and Guinier. Indeed, it is this lingering and epic guilt of our slavo-colonial experience that cognitively throws some Africans off-balance and prompts them to make such peevish and lame statements as the African having purportedly gleefully collaborated in his or her own enslavement.

Indeed, as Daniel P. Mannix and Malcolm Cowley write in their classic treatise on this subject, titled ***Black Cargoes***, the process of African enslavement, as one may also aptly presume for all other such forms of exploitation, involved the wealthy and powerful. And the proportion, or percentage, of the latter among the general population was, needless to say, few and far between.

And so contrary to what Professor Henry Louis Gates, Jr., would have the rest of the world believe, Africans are no sub-human species perpetually poised towards committing untold atrocities against one another. Indeed, the collaborative enslavement of Africans by some elite Africans and their proto-capitalist European counterparts, has myriad parallels in global human history, including the enslavement of the ancient Hebrews in Egypt, as well as the near-annihilation of European Jewry by Adolf Hitler's Nazi Germany. In the Bible, for instance, we are apprised of the barbarous fact that it was the very elder siblings of Joseph who sold their younger brother to the Arabs, who in turn took the future Egyptian prime minister into the land of purported Jewish misery and captivity. And here also, it is significant to observe that the Biblical narrative regarding the enslavement of Jews specifically names the Arabs, not indigenous Africans, as the major collaborators. Yet, interestingly enough, Skip Gates had the temerity and abject effrontery to highlight the Magen David (or Star of David) in the background of his 1994 (or was it 1995?) ***New York Times*** article in which the Harvard University African Studies professor callously and ignobly labeled then-ailing and aging autodidact scholar, Professor John Henrik Clarke "a pseudo-scholar."

And since he appears to be so pathologically obsessed with the Jewish State of Israel, for whatever capriciously personal reasons, as Professor Mazrui aptly points out, for in his "Wonders of the African World" Gates enters Tanzania—and the African continent, for that matter—through Tel Aviv or Jerusalem, it would also be quite refreshing and even morally edifying if Skip Gates could also embark on another project titled "Wonders of the Jewish World," for example, in which the Harvard poster-boy of African-American prosperity meticulously documents Jewish participation in both the Holocaust and the latter's pharaonic experience in Egypt. Such a project would undoubtedly be worthwhile, in view of the fact that not long ago another Harvard scholar published a massive tome unreservedly condemning all Germans for having eagerly and mirthfully participated in the massive enslavement and massacre of German and European Jewry.

23

As the great traditional African thinkers observed eons ago, the Billy goat is a very strange species of anti-social animal that capriciously gloats on his unique ability to defecate in the otherwise antiseptic village square and, by so doing, repugnantly blight the idyllic landscape of culture and civility. Of course, we all know that the Billy goat is just a poignant metaphor for those among our human species who have elected the collective humiliation, or discredit, of their people as the domain in which to careeristically or professionally distinguish themselves. And on this score, perhaps, no single global African human being deserves the nonesuch accolade of ***Pope Billy Goat I*** more than Harvard University's Professor Henry Louis Gates, Jr. Interestingly, one may aptly add, the Billy Goat is a metaphorical species of contradictions, though such contradiction may be seen to be more of one which entails intellectual and moral myopia than sheer esthetic finesse or genius. For at the very moment that the Billy Goat disdainfully lifts up his right hind-leg to defecate in the village square, which invariably doubles as a makeshift town-hall, the square is always filled to capacity. And what is more, being a caudate quadruped, the Billy Goat is innately incapable of cleaning its anal orifice. The embarrassing result is that legions of flies swarm his rump and force him to seek asylum in the herbal hedges or his kraal, if he happens to be in domestic captivity. But what is even more interesting about this anti-social quadruped is its impudent ability to chomp its proverbial cake—in this context, his tuft of elephant grass—and also have it, as it were.

In short, Piedmont and Cambridge, Massachusetts', own Mr. Henry Louis Gates, Jr., has set up a trap for continental Africans and their African-Caribbean kin that threatens to strangle the culprit himself. In other words, our "indigenous" African-American guru has tragically and pathetically set himself up on a suicidal course. And while he cannot blame anybody for hoisting with his own petard, as it were, we, nevertheless, sympathize with the culprit. But, unfortunately, that is about all that we can do in the offing or foreseeable future. Indeed, we intend to proffer the impenitent Aryan surrogate an immeasurable span of rope-o—noose—with which to hang himself. We shall simply not stay around as witnesses or abettors; that way, nobody can accuse or charge us with misprision or any capital offense. Nonetheless, we also intend to be present at his funeral, if the godforsaken misanthrope's family determines to accord him one. But true to character, don't count on any of us to eulogize our renowned "distant cousin," for the latter burden belongs to his friends and immediate relatives, particularly the Aryan-American man and his womenfolk, as well as their beneficent extended family in England who leeringly sponsored our inveterate internal enemy's so-called WONDERS OF THE AFRICAN WORLD. We just intend to be present at the culprit's funeral in order to ascertain his official demise as well as to ensure that he does not resurrect, like the Christ of Nazareth, to deal us even more sanguinary mayhem or carnage.

Even so, we hereby happily announce our irredentist triumph in the glaring intellectual and historiographical exposure of Harvard University's Professor Henry Louis Gates, Jr. And here, it may be recalled that the latter, for more than two decades, has embarked on a systematic expropriation of continental African heritage, evidently with the same motive employed by the Western European slavo-colonial architects regarding ancient Egypt and the entire Nile Valley region of East Africa, as well as the East African littoral. Thus, in his otherwise brilliant, and even sterling, Jefferson Memorial Lectures to the august United States Library of Congress in the year 2002, the West Virginian native had the temerity to magisterially claim the famous continental African woman poet Ms. Phillis Wheatley as the first major "indigenous" African-American poet. In recalling the 1772 epic trial and oral examination of Ms. Wheatley by some of the greatest politicians and esthetic wits of the Massachusetts colony to authenticate this continental African woman's authorship of her seminal volume of poetry, titled *Poems on Various Subjects, Religious and Moral*, Professor Henry Louis Gates, Jr., declared rather triumphantly: "And so, against the greatest odds, *Poems on Various Subjects, Religious and Moral*, became the first book of poetry published by a person of African descent in the English language, marking the beginning of an African American literary tradition."

Nothing, regarding the preceding quote, could be farther from the truth; this is in no way to either hint or assert that the remarkable scholastic output of the Oxbridge alumnus has been meticulously about the business of truth or authenticity. It is simply to elicit the virtual house-of-cards that Gatesian scholarship has regrettably become nowadays. For starters, the poet Phillis Wheatley, who is widely celebrated by many a global African woman intellectual and literary scholar or artist, was far more than just "a person of African descent." To be certain, Ms. Wheatley was born on the African continent, the very land-mass whose inhabitants or citizens Mr. Henry Louis Gates, Jr., has disdainfully and emphatically described as his "distant relatives." So how come that all of a sudden, the chief-constable of Harvard University's department of African-American Studies is hailing Ms. Wheatley, our continental African poet laureate, as "a person of African descent"? The answer is simple: Mr. Gates has elected to serve as a mainstream American surrogate missionary of continental African expropriation. His main and bounden objective is to surveil the disciplines of African Literature and Culture and ensure that nothing worthy of our intellectual while is duly credited to the perennially humiliated and globally maligned continental African.

Indeed, as Professor Gates is himself cognizant, Ms. Wheatley was imported by white slavocrats into the United States from continental Africa. The poet was about six or seven years old at the time of her capture and enslavement. It is also certain that she spoke an African language, not the English of "indigenous" African-Americans. Ms. Wheatley did not speak any European language, though she would later be taught Latin and other "high-culture" European languages once her remarkable genius became apparent to members of the white Wheatley family of Boston. It is also interesting to observe that while the slaver or ship that brought her into the United States had weighed anchor at the Port of Goree, in present-day Senegal, the celebrated future poet could have hailed from any part of the West African littoral, or the so-called Gulf of Guinea. My nationalist pride invariably prompts me to assert that Ms. Wheatley most likely was a Gold Coaster (or Ghanaian) of Akan extraction. Why I am so insistently prompted regarding the ethnic or cultural provenance of Ms. Wheatley's, I have no idea, except to conclude that it is the voice of our ancestors prodding me in such direction. And this is no total accident, for a generation or two before Ms. Wheatley, another Gold Coaster, Wilhem Anton Amo (a.k.a. William Anthony Amo[h]) had been taken to Germany and educated by the German royal family. Unlike the far less fortunate Ms. Wheatley, Dr. William Anthony Amo[h] would rise among the august ranks of the prestigious German professoriate and even be named a convocational marshall at some of the most elite universities of Deutschland. Indeed, in 1994, while I was teaching at the Indiana State University at Terra Haute, a senior colleague with whom I team-taught continental African history, Dr. Richard V. Pierard, participated in a Christian theological conference in Germany and heartily reported having personally viewed a statuary bust of this great, pioneering Gold Coaster. Indeed, so patriotic and Afrocentric was Professor William Anthony Amo[h] that he was to later return to the land of his ancestry and live out the twilight of his career and existence. A reliable source once informed this writer that Dr. Amoh's grave is located in the village of Shama, in the Western Region of Ghana. Like Benjamin Banneker, whom the former preceded by a few decades, Professor Amo[h] was described as a "sidereal speculator," or "stargazer," which simply meant that he had a remarkable knowledge of the physical sciences. Somewhere among the considerable corpus of his writings, Professor Henry Louis Gates, Jr., has recorded that Ghana's Dr. William Anthony Amo[h] wrote what may be regarded as approximating the first treatise or dissertation on modern psychology. Unfortunately, while the title of his dissertation is widely known, having been initially reported by Swiss scholar and anthropologist Janheinz Jahn, its exact contents are reportedly lost. It is not known or clear whether Dr. Amo[h] returned to the Gold Coast with his dissertation, or some smart alecky European intellectual simply squirreled it and deftly incorporated its contents into his mediocre scholarship which the latter than passed off as his own, a not-so-impossible or improbable contingency.

Interestingly, like his "race-woman" Phillis Wheatley, whom he preceded by at least one generation, Dr. William Anthony Amo[h] also distinguished himself in the literary sub-genre of poetry, having also written epic panegyrics extolling the majestic dignity of the German monarch. Maybe this esthetic kinship is what prompts me to insist that Ms. Wheatley was more likely a Ghanaian, of Akan extraction, possibly a Fante, than a Senegalese. It has often been said that poets are kindred souls; so maybe being a poet myself has endowed me with the kind of intuitive, investigative and inquisitive insight or flair that may not be readily accessible to the non-poet

24

Among the Akan of Ghana and Cote d'Ivoire and elsewhere within the West African sub-region and, of course, the Diaspora, there is a saying that: "It is the sagacious [or an intelligent] person who is usually dispatched as an envoy [or emissary] in matters of gravity, not the giant-gaited or loose-jointed." In its Akan original, it reads: "Yesoma Oba Nyansafo, na yennsoma annamon tenten." In sum, in dispatching Professor Henry Louis Gates, Jr., to undertake his epic travelogue titled *Wonders of the African World*, the messenger's magnanimous sponsors—both the British Broadcasting Corporation (BBC-TV) and America's Public Broadcasting System (PBS-TV)—could not have done both their renowned messenger and themselves any worse; for the former precipitously lost his scholastic credibility, a prized commodity in academia which the Harvard denizen is not likely to regain or recover in the foreseeable future.

What makes the situation even more pathetic is the fact that prior to his acceptance of his assignment, the Piedmont, West Virginia, native knew fully well that he had not adequately prepared himself for the task. In other words, while Professor Gates is incontrovertibly a leading light in African-American literary criticism or scholarship, the man had done only marginal work in the area of African history, culture and politics. Unfortunately, his fame and great fortune in the sub-discipline of African-American Studies deluded the W. E. B. DuBois Professor of the Humanities into presuming himself to be equally authoritative in the aforementioned area of global African personality studies. That the author-narrator of *Wonders of the African World* was to shortly acknowledge this woeful deficiency in the wake of the heated controversy which met with his travelogue, evinced a paradoxical admixture of intellectual honesty and dishonesty. And here, also, it must be poignantly observed that Mr. Gates took on the overwhelming or behemoth demands of his project because caught in the heady throes of his vaulting ambitions, he had, against all odds, convinced himself of being the best person for the job. And true to his well-calibrated pre-determination, the best man for the job he was. For his *Wonders of the African World* is, perhaps, the greatest act of betrayal among any group of the human species.

On another level, however, his decision to collaborate with continental Africa's Western detractors in the striking vein of a Judas Iscariot, was a great blessing in disguise for the rest of us. The preceding, coupled with Mr. Gates' dastardly attempt at driving a lethal wedge between continental Africans and African-Americans, has almost certainly ensured that his literary scholarship on global Africans has to be promptly and drastically revised. For instance, in the Fall of 2003, at the Harvard Black Alumni confabulation, the chairman of that flagship academy's department of African-American Studies insisted that continental African immigrants and their first-, and even second-, generation children ought to be sharply distinguished from a group that he designated "indigenous" African-Americans. The motive was purely political; and it was to ensure that the undergraduate children of recent African immigrants at Ivy League institution would be systematically accorded short-shrift treatment, by drastically reducing their purportedly, uncomfortably and undesirably massive presence at these institutions. The sole crime of the children of these immigrants is that their ancestors had "deviously" escaped plantational slavery which, according to Professors Gates and Guinier, is the ineluctable lot of global Africans. On this score, therefore, the Gatesian-Guinierian call for continental African and Caribbean excision from the Ivy League establishment may be squarely seen to have a racial edge to it. For a similar call has yet to be issued regarding such equally, and perhaps even more, prominent groups as Asian-and Latin-Americans, and even recent European immigrants, from both East and West.

Pertaining to the need for Professor Gates to promptly and drastically revise his literary theory, we have in mind such seminal literary lights as Phillis Wheatley and Gustavus Vassa. Regarding the former, Professor Gates told an eminent gathering of Americans in the august Library of Congress in 2002 that the continental African-born Ms. Wheatley was "the first person of African descent" to publish a book of poetry in the English language here in the United States, thus "marking the beginning of an African American literary tradition." The preceding remark, it may be recalled, was registered on the momentous occasion of the annual Jefferson Memorial Lectures. At the aforementioned Harvard University Black Alumni confabulation, Mr. Gates, staunchly backed by Ms. Lani Guinier, insisted that an African-American is only one all of whose four grandparents had toiled as slaves here in the United States. Going by their own assessment, Ms. Wheatley, a purebred and African-born American does not qualify to be reckoned as African-American. At best, Professor Gates might find it more comfortable, and even convenient, to categorize Ms. Wheatley as his "distant relative," just as he said of us continental African-born Americans in the wake of the telecast of his hatchet travelogue, ***Wonders of the African World***.

And here, also, it may be aptly recalled that Ms. Wheatley, that was not her real name, arrived in the United States, at Boston, to be precise, as a fragile six-year-old. In all likelihood, she spoke a West African language; it has been suggested that perhaps Ms. Wheatley spoke Wolof, the predominant language of the Senegambia region where the ship which ferried her across the saline graveyard of the Atlantic Ocean embarked her. But, perhaps, what is even more significant is the fact that Phillis Wheatley never envisaged herself as an African-American," much less an American citizen, in spite of the historical fact that she had been treated far more generously than the bulk of her ilk. Even in some of the poems in which she appears to gloat over the fact of being forcibly introduced into a relatively more intellectually and culturally exciting Western civilization, Ms. Wheatley also notes the fact that she had been callously torn away from her loving continental African family, a psychical torment which she endured throughout her short existence here in the United States. And yet, in his ***Wonders of the African World***, Professor Gates makes it seem as if every continental African who found himself, or herself for that matter, enslaved in the so-called New World had been automatically sold by his or her kinsmen and women. And even though Ms. Wheatley had written verse extolling her relatively good fortune, for having supposedly been rescued out of cultural and spiritual benightment, in all probability, such obviously embarrassing and self-alienating deployment of diction was engaged more as a strategic act of survival in a bestial, capitalist slavocracy, than a visceral expression of gratitude for having been allowed to live her patently miserable existence among a bunch of imperious troglodytes. And so Professor Gates would have to go back to his archives and mount a fresh and vigorous search for an "indigenous" African-American literary pioneer.

It is also interesting and significant to observe that Ms. Wheatley arrived in the United States from Africa in 1768. Exactly a century later, African-Americans would be granted nominal citizenship by White America. In sum, even if she had desired the temporally unenviable offer of American citizenship, Ms. Wheatley would have had to wait another century or be reincarnated in order to be able to accept such thankless gesture. In sum, continental Africans hereby assert, in no uncertain terms, our intention to fiercely protect the Africanity of our literary matriarch. Maybe the BBC and PBS would help Professor Gates to undertake another equally dear or expensive travelogue in the latter's search for an "indigenous" African-American Phillis Wheatley. He may even decide to start his journey from Downtown Dublin.

Furthermore, Professor Gates told his predominantly White-American audience at the Library of Congress: "With the publication of her book, Phillis

Wheatley, almost immediately, became the most famous African on the face of the earth, the Oprah Winfrey of her time. Phillis was the toast of London, where she had been sent with Nathaniel Wheatley in the summer [of 1773] to oversee the publication of her book." Indeed, by clearly acknowledging her unalloyed Africanity, Skip Gates contradicts his own submission, or argument, seeking to establish Phillis Wheatley as the undisputed matriarch of Black poetry in the United States. And here, we solemnly recall that on the crest of the human rights revolution during the 1960s, firebrand activist-warrior Malcolm X constantly and consistently exhorted "indigenous" African-Americans that: "You cannot hate Africa [and Africans] and not hate yourself." Skip Gates seems to prefer being characterized as a "Head-Negro-In-Charge"; and on the latter score, he must not be begrudged or deprived.

In fact, so execrable, or loathsome, did America appear to Wheatley that in her celebrated poem titled "To the Right Honourable William, Earl of Dartmouth," this West African poet of genius lamented the fact that a cruel and steely-hearted European slaver would tear her away from the loving "breasts" of her parents, as well as "from *Afric's* fancy'd happy seat," much the same manner as the great autobiographer-memoirist Olaudah Equaino (or Gustavus Vassa), her contemporary, would disconsolately lament the ineffable depravity of the Trans-Atlantic Slave Trade. And so, where Professor Henry Louis Gates, Jr., prefers to see the African as a benighted slavocrat, those who had a first-hand experience of this catastrophic event disconsolately lament the fact of being callously wrenched away from an idyllic civil existence into the indescribable nightmare that encapsulated the proverbial continental African experience in the so-called New World.

25

When this series began, a little over five months ago, it was intended to be limited in scope to the direly controversial issue which it sought to address. The issue regarded a 2003 annual conference of Black Harvard University alumni during which session several prominent African-American intellectuals, including Professors Henry Louis Gates, Jr., and Lani Guinier, intimated their utter perturbation, as well as displeasure, at what the latter Harvard faculty members termed as the over-representation of continental African and African-Caribbean undergraduate students in that august, flagship academy at the purported expense of African-American students. The very categorization by Professors Gates and Guinier of Black students into the children of "immigrants" and "indigenes" was one that raised a lot of curious questions; this is because their label of "immigrant" regarded Black undergraduate students whose parents, rather than these students themselves, had not been born in the United States. In effect, to Professors Gates and Guinier, it appeared that the historically and politically significant fact that the Black children of recent immigrants who had themselves been born and raised right here in the United States, had no legitimacy in terms of their right to citizenship or the franchise. This grim state of affairs even became more complicated when the same attempt at summary judicial proscription was extended to the children of African-Caribbeans, many of whom were either contemporaries of their proscribers or even much older. Some of these so-called recent African-Caribbean immigrants had actually been born right here in the United States; but even more importantly, remarkable numbers among their ranks had served in such militarily troubled terrains as Vietnam, Korea and the Persian Gulf. In most instances, their first-generation immigrant parents had lived in this country for at least a half-generation before the births of their critics, whose octogenarian parents were their contemporaries. The sole grounds for their civic proscription, or citizenship disqualification, or more specifically their major crime, was the fact that their parents and grandparents had not been born as chattel slaves on one of the many infamous Southern plantations right here in the United States.

So in essence, the Gatesian-Guinierian test of ethnic and civic authenticity is simply a contest among historical victims, in which those who perceive themselves to have been the most victimized, pretty much arrogate themselves the right of citizenship conferral, or lack thereof, on the purportedly less victimized. The logic, as was eloquently depicted in Professor Henry Louis Gates, Jr's marathon documentary Eurocentrically and flamboyantly titled *Wonders of the African World*, is that any recent continental African immigrant in the United States perforce had an ancestor who willfully and delightfully participated in the brutal enslavement of African-Americans. This rather sophomoric, to speak much less of the patently unscientific, logic falls flat on its face when African-Caribbeans are corralled into the equation. For starters, as both Professors Gates and Guinier are fully cognizant of, African-Caribbeans have endured the triple sociopolitical and cultural bane of slavery, colonialism and, currently, like most of their continental African kin, neocolonialism, even as African-Americans traversed the unmitigably savage and barbaric terrains of chattel slavery, Jim Crowism and, presently, de facto and de jure second-class citizenship status.

Ever since the current series logically evolved into a running and comprehensive critique of Professor Gates' filmic documentary titled *Wonders of the African World*, I have come across caches of Internet documents regarding a vigorous but not necessarily totally salutary debate that largely took place some four years ago, on the question of both the historiographical accuracy and ideological validity of Professor Gates' *Wonders of the African World*. One such document is authored by the author-narrator of the aforementioned documentary. Titled, rather predictably, "A Preliminary Response To Ali Mazrui's Preliminary Critique of 'Wonders of the African World,'" the renowned author and Harvard University professor of African-American Studies rather disingenuously welcomes the critical ferment which swelled up in the wake of his *Wonders'* broadcast by BBC-Television and PBS-Television, the major sponsors of the aforementioned documentary. "I am first and last a teacher, and anytime [that] so many people are moved to discuss and debate African history must be seen as a good time…. We are, after all, scholars, not devotees of a religion or an ideology, and the exchange of ideas without vilification or name-calling is one of the fundamental [hallmarks] of the scholar's calling" (*West African Review* [2000] ISSN 1525-4488).

Indeed, anybody who has studiously followed the Gatesian *Wonders*, as depicted in the documentary in question, readily recognizes the vituperative and offensive narratological style adopted by the West Virginian native as nothing more than beggarly or mean-spirited. But what is even more amusing, if also because it reeks of the pathologically presumptuous, is that Gates envisages himself as a pioneer—or missionary frontiersman—vis-à-vis the evolution and development of post-colonial African political history. Consequently, he glibly writes:

"Like so many of my contemporaries in African and African American Studies, I came of age in the early sixties, just as many African countries were gaining their independence. I was ten years old in 1960, that great year of African independence, and for reasons I do not understand, I busied myself memorizing the names of each African country, its capital, and its leader, pronouncing their names as closely as I could to the way [in which the] evening news commentator did on the nightly news." For a self-confessed child prodigy who started college at 16 or 17 years old, to Skip Gates' assertion that he was at a total loss as to why he memorized the names of newly-independent African countries and their leaders, we must all hasten to say "Amen" to it; for it is doubtful whether he could have come up with any constructive reason or reasons even if Mr. Gates had attempted to avail himself of any. Indeed, chances are that at the time of composing his rather elaborate preliminary rejoinder to Professor Ali A. Mazrui's earlier critique, Skip Gates had come to the definitive conclusion that any good reasons that the proud Piedmont, Virginia, native might have harbored for Africa and continental Africans, in general, must have been grossly mistaken or even outright flagitious, to speak much less of the patently flagrant.

The renowned ***Signifying Monkey*** theorist also exhibits his inimitable mastery of hyperbole. For instance, he writes that he spent the 1970-1971 academic year living in an Ujamaa village in President Julius Nyerere's Tanzania. And here, the critical reader is readily apprised of the fact that "an academic year" is just another theatrical way of saying nine months. But, of course, as has become a salient hallmark of his, Mr. Gates underestimates the mensural capacity of his audience and so he further notes: "After an extended time at Kilimatinde, I moved to Dar Es Salaam, where I lived for two months, then hitch-hiked across the equator, managing to travel from Tanzania through Kenya, Uganda, Rwanda and the Congo, by land and by river, from the Indian Ocean to the Atlantic Ocean without leaving the ground. By the age of 20, I had travelled through nine African countries, saddened only that an illness [,] a severe case of dysentery [,] had] prevented me from fulfilling another dream, which was to cross the Sahara by land."

Needless to say, we cannot but only heartily congratulate Uncle Skippy for being such a good tourist and precocious explorer in the quite enviable tradition of Henry Morton Stanley and Sir Richard Burton, Gates' historiographical authority on the Niger. It is also quite interesting that in the very next paragraph, the abruptly awestruck Mr. Gates fawningly—or is obsequiously?—credits Professor Soyinka and the former's longtime buddy Mr. Kwame Anthony Appiah for having virtually shaped him into the W. E. B. DuBois Humanities and African-

American Studies professor that he is today at Harvard University. Interestingly, however, not quite awhile ago, in a magazine or journal article in which he detailed his meteoric and phenomenal rise as an undergraduate at Yale and later a doctoral student at Cambridge, the "distant cousin" of continental Africans barely mentioned Professor Soyinka; his putative doppelganger, Dr. Kwame Anthony [I have since learned that his "Anthony" is an Anglo-corrupted variation of the Akan-Ghanaian name *Ntori*] Appiah did not even get a passing mention. Back then, Gates credited a White-American Yale University professor, who supervised his undergraduate thesis on some godforsaken Eurocentric subject, with having almost wholly been responsible for his very successful academic career. In the same article, the proud author of "Colored People" gave the curious impression that Professor Soyinka had been more than grateful to have had Uncle Skippy as his student, because the authorities at Cambridge University had pretty much determined that the future, pioneering African Nobel literature laureate had no place in the august portals of that globally revered Oxbridge academy. In sum, like Eshu, the Yoruba trickster-god that he so eloquently dissertates about in his well-received but rarely read "Signifying Monkey," ideological Gatesianism is no respecter of principles, except to simply follow the direction of the wind, depending on the season and time of day.

The preceding notwithstanding, perhaps the most disturbing thing about the impudent Gatesian antics is the fact that its mercurial choreographer invariably finds a ready scapegoat in the august and revered personage of Professor Wole Soyinka. Regarding his putatively pathological hatred for Africa and its people, Gates unctuously gushes: "Soyinka taught me many things, far too many to detail here…. 'Criticism, like charity, he would repeat, again and again like a mantra, 'starts at home.' And so, in the pages of the journal, Transition, on whose editorial board I have sat since 1973, Soyinka attacked the excesses of brutal dictators such as Idi Amin, Mobutu, or Sani Abacha, as well as the reluctance of other African and African-American intellectuals to do so in public and somehow, of giving comfort to colonialists, racists, or neocolonialists. Since graduate school, I have taken Soyinka's notion of 'tough love' as the ultimate sign of [the] true commitment that a scholar can demonstrate in his devotion to her or his field."

Here again, needless to say, we find it absolutely unnecessary to second-guess Professor Soyinka as to why he appears not to have tutored his former student on the practiced discipline that ought to be inextricably coupled with the otherwise sterling art of dispassionate albeit sensitive and respectable scholarship, which Professor Soyinka has been globally known to practice with inimitable finesse (Read, for instance, Soyinka's play titled *A Dance of the Forests*). For it goes without saying that "tough love" cannot be equated with the psychotic ritual of cutting one's nose in order to spite one's face, as it were. And if, indeed, Skip Gates is telling us the truth, then, perhaps, he needs to go back to Professor Soyinka for further lessons, for the author of **Loose Canons** appears to have grossly misunderstood his mentor, or he has simply learned the wrong things from somebody else whose identity he confuses with Professor Soyinka's.

26

In his so-called preliminary response to Professor Ali Mazrui's admittedly mordant critique of the filmic documentary titled **Wonders of the African World**, Harvard University's Professor Henry Louis Gates, Jr., claims rather peevishly that his widely discredited documentary aimed at vehemently debunking the protracted and persistent denial by European scholars that ancient Egyptian civilization was the veritably "hybrid" fabrication of both continental African and Asian peoples. If so, then such apparently proactive initiative comes as rather too little and too late; and, indeed, one wonders why it took this pseudo-pioneering historiographical irredentist so long. And the answer, here, is not very difficult to figure out: Professor Gates spent most of the 1980s, when he was a steadily rising star, debunking the phenomenal technological and cultural achievements of indigenous Africans, both in ancient Egypt as well as in the so-called sub-Saharan Africa. At one point, as already noted in an earlier installment of this series, Skip Gates impugned the historical validity of such flagship medieval Malian academies as Sankore and Timbuktu, and even mocked at the fact of the historical existence of such prolific scholars as Ahmed Baba and Mahmud Kati. He even denounced the late Professor John Henrik Clarke, of the Harlem School of pioneering Afrocentrists, as the veritable essence of pseudo-scholarship in the Op-Ed pages of the **New York Times**. And so for those of us who have been studiously following the exuberant, but not necessarily constructive, campus-hopping career of Mr. Gates, it was quite amusing to watch the man, pop-eyed, being conducted through the great, well-stocked medieval library at Timbuktu.

Not surprisingly, the apparently insuperable cynic in Uncle Skippy got the better part of the Keyser, West Virginia, native as he came out of the edifice and panned his digital camera onto a vista of a medieval Timbuktu street, declaring his utter disappointment that the place did not look nearly as impressive as the mythopoeic accounts that he had devoured in grade-school history textbooks. Indeed, had he acquired any substantive knowledge about the Euro-Aryan forces, as well as the decadent internal political forces that descended on Mali in the post-Musa era, and later, he would, almost certainly, not have registered such blisteringly sophomoric disappointment. It was almost as if the middle-aged Harvard egghead expected African history to have frozen in its tracks over the turbulent course of the last three centuries until his recent rediscovery.

Further, the W. E. B. DuBois professor of African-American Studies does not help matters in observing sheepishly that he was not professionally equal to the humongous epistemological facility which the production of his pseudo-epic documentary required. To the preceding effect, the author-narrator of **Wonders of the African World** plaintively observes: "Let me state the obvious: I am a professor of literature, not an historian, an archeologist or an anthropologist. Accordingly, the Wall-to-Wall Production Company and I consulted with a wide range of scholars to shape my approach to this vast and complex subject, on both the film series and the book that accompanies it. I have attached, at the end of this piece, a list of some of the scholars whom I consulted."

Immediately upon reading the preceding quote, I consulted the aforementioned list of consultants for **Wonders of the African World**. And since I was very interested in the filmic episode on the Asante of Ghana, I went straight to that section of the list. Among the purported consultants was listed a Professor John Aquandah, to whose name was appended the credential: "Authority on early Akan history of Ghana." I promptly hit the Internet for verification, because the only Ghanaian archeologist that I knew had a similar sounding name; however, he was neither called "John" nor "Aquandah." The veteran archeologist and sometime Radio Ghana History Lecturer was called Professor James Anquandah; and lo and behold, when I clicked on "Google.com" and entered James Anquandah, the man that I have known since I was in the third grade at the University of Ghana's Staff Village Primary School, during the late 1960s and early 1970s, popped up. And while he may not personally remember me, I knew Professor James Anquandah pretty well, though a little more than thirty years later, I am not quite certain whether I would be readily able to recognize the man if I saw him today. I knew Professor Anquandah quite well because I used to hang around the Archeology Department of the University of Ghana, at Legon, most afternoons during lunch time and sometimes after three o'clock, in the afternoon, when school was over and I had to wait for my father to take me home. My father was the Technical Director in the School of Music and Drama, now re-designated the School for the Performing Arts. The latter school was housed as a semi-autonomous division of the world-renowned Institute of African Studies whose founding director was Professor J. H. Kwabena Nketia, an equally world-renowned continental African musicologist. I frequented the Archeology Department at Legon viewing human remains with a classmate, David Bulla Marmata, whose father, Dr. Marmata, was director of the Institute of Adult Education, which was housed next to the Archeology Department. I was also the best history pupil in my class, and so it was no wonder that I would frequent the fossil glass cases in Professor Anquandah's department. I don't quite remember in what specific academic capacity he served, except that I found him to be quite an enigmatic figure, having been taught by my grandparents that graveyards were among the most sacred sites on earth, and also that the deliberate desecration of graveyards spelled dire consequences for both the culprit and a condoning society. And then here I was in a university department where people trained in order to engage in exactly the kinds of activities that bode ill for the continuous survival of the very fabric of Ghanaian society.

Indeed, it may be deemed rather trivial that Professor Gates would glaringly misidentify Professor James Anquandah as John Aquandah; for an obscure community college instructor like me, such error may be deemed quite pardonable even if equally unacceptable, but for a flamboyant Ivy League scholar like Professor Henry Louis Gates, Jr., such significant error verges on the outright criminal. It is indisputably tantamount to sloppy scholarship.

Other expert consultants on the Asante section of Professor Gates' list include the late Professor Mawere Opoku, an African music and dance specialist of genius and my deceased father's avuncular friend and colleague. And here, also, one may seriously question the presence of Professor Opoku on this list, since Skip Gates neither discussed Asante music nor dance in his documentary series; and neither was Professor Opoku brought on camera to engage in any discussion on some of the most critical questions raised by Skip Gates in his "African Wonders," being that Professor Opoku, an elderly Asante chief and scholar, knew far more about the culture in question than any of the other consultants thereon listed. Among the latter are Dr. Tom McCaskie, of Birmingham, England; Dr. Akosua Perbi, a Fulbright scholar, whom Professor Gates wickedly and callously exposed to global ridicule; Professor John Fynn, of the University of Ghana; and Professor Adu Boahen, whom Skip Gates describes as an "authority on Asante history," and perhaps the best-known West African historian, who, it may be recalled, was interviewed by Professor Ali A. Mazrui in his 1986 series titled *The Africans: A Triple Heritage*. And here, it is also significant to note that almost no Anglophone West African high school graduate who majored in history has never heard the name of Professor A. Adu Boahen. In fact, most of the latter's books are used as texts in most Ghanaian and West African high schools and universities.

Interestingly, Professor Gates chose not to use the input of the most significant and distinguished academic expert on Asante history, the first African head of the University of Ghana's Department of History, as well as the sometime invested Royal Historian of the Asante nation under His Majesty, King Opoku Ware II. Instead, Skip Gates chose to interview Dr. Akosua Perbi, a very intelligent but far less knowlegeable specialist on indigenous or domestic slavery in the West African sub-region. Needless to say, the problem raised by this approach to historiography is readers and spectators were seriously shortchanged. It may also be significantly noted that at the time of shooting his *Wonders of the African World*, Dr. Perbi had just defended her doctoral dissertation on indigenous West African slavery, a study which largely focused on Ghana, a significant market in the Trans-Atlantic Slave Trade, but scarcely the most significant market on the West African coast. Interestingly, however, Professor Gates decided not to film in perhaps the most significant market of the Trans-Atlantic Slave Trade, the area designated the Slave Coast, which spanned parts of modern Benin and most of the post-colonial Nigerian littoral. Instead, Dr. Gates has glibly offered the presence of infamous Nigerian military dictator General Sani Abacha, at the helm of the political affairs of the most populous post-colonial African country, as a valid scholastic excuse for declining to film a portion of his *Wonders of the African World* in that economically, culturally and politically cutthroat West African polity. Needless to say, we intend to provide, in due course, the real reason why Professor Gates elected this curious intellectual approach to West African history, particularly vis-à-vis the intractable question of continental African participation in the massive enslavement of the people who eventually became known as *Negroes, Blacks, Colored, Afro-Americans* and *African-Americans*.

Indeed, excepting Nigeria from the controversial and ineluctable equation of the Trans-Atlantic Slave Trade, as Professor Gates does with his *Wonders of the African World*, is akin to being conferred with a doctoral degree in British Literature by the University of Cambridge without the recipient having heard the name of the immortalized William Shakespeare, the Bard-of-Avon.

Indeed, while we have respectfully disagreed with Professor Ali A. Mazrui, regarding some of his critical comments on Professor Gates' *Wonders of the African World*, we must, nonetheless, humbly and honestly agree with the leading Kenyan political scientist on the fact of the latter's dead-on accuracy in impugning the salient motives for Skip Gates' gaping omission of Nigeria's critical and massive contribution to the evolution and development of African history, even while also emphatically and categorically recognizing our patent ideological divergence on the same question. On this score, we also question why having definitively recognized his irreconcilably vast intellectual and ideological differences with Skip Gates, Professor Mazrui, nevertheless, persisted in rapturously patronizing a subject whose phenomenal intellectual productivity redounded to the cultural, political and philosophical regression of global African development, especially in the critical area of Trans-Atlantic collaborative solidarity. We make the preceding observation based on the fact that the distinguished Kenyan political scientist was fully aware of his moral and epistemological differences with Professor Gates when Dr. Mazrui eagerly offered to pen a blurb for the book accompanying the former's documentary titled *Wonders of the African World*. Exactly what "wonders" did Professor Mazrui expect of his inveterate intellectual nemesis when he "graciously" offered to write his blurb for Skip Gates? Indeed, it is squarely on this score that we are inclined to agreeing with some of the critical questions raised by Professor Wole Soyinka (see "The Problem With You, Ali Mazrui! Response to Ali's Millennial 'Conclusion'—*West Africa Review* [2000] ISSN: 1525-4488) regarding his longtime Kenyan archnemesis' motives in mordantly lighting into the Gatesian *Wonders of the African World*.

Initially, Professor Mazrui claims to have drafted a blurb which read: "Is this book a portrayal of Africa, or does it mirror the soul of one of its lost sons, Henry Louis Gates, Jr? Gates' talent for both stimulation and irritation is brilliantly at work in these pages. You must read this work and then look back in anger!" The final draft which appeared on the back-cover of the textbook accompaniment to *Wonders of the African World*, reads: "This is more than a book about Africa. It is a study in black America's profound ambivalence about our shared ancestral continent. Caught between a distaste for Africa within his own family and his abiding love for and fascination with Africa, Henry Louis Gates, Jr., traverses the continent with a keen eye, a brilliant mind and an ambivalent heart."

Needless to say, the latter quote, which constitutes a blurb on the textbook version of *Wonders of the African World*, tersely and inimitably encapsulates the essence of both Gatesian ideological media. And it is this, more than any other, reason why we could not agree more with those who exhorted Dr. Mazrui's constructive quietude on the Gatesian wonders (see Mazrui's "'Wonders of the African World' by Henry Louis Gates, Jr.: A Preliminary Critique of the TV Series"). Lighting into both the author and his work, we are inclined to partially agree with Professor Soyinka, amounted to an otiose overkill. It also reeks of blatant belligerence by proxy, or proximal vitriol, since it was Professor Soyinka, rather than Skip Gates, who caustically carped Dr. Mazrui's 1986 filmic documentary titled *The Africans: A Triple Heritage*. Back then, as we vividly recall, the newly-knighted, pioneering African Nobel Literature Laureate characterized *The Africans* as "a half-way house." It was also the first time that this writer learned of the long-standing bad blood between these two distinguished African intellectual artists. As Chinua Achebe would wittily say: "It is morning yet on creation day.

27

Among the scholars who remarkably contributed to the vigorous debate sparked by Professor Henry Louis Gates' filmic documentary titled **Wonders of the African World,** were Professors Amechi A. Okolo and Joseph Inikori, both of whose names prompt this writer to presume their Nigerian identity and nationality. In his quite instructive and edifying article titled "My Preliminary Response To: 'A Preliminary Response to Ali Mazrui's Preliminary Critique,'" an obvious titular take on Professor Gates' rejoinder to the latter's arch-nemesis, Professor Ali A. Mazrui, Professor Amechi Okolo aptly observes the fact that the sticky question of continental African participation in the enslavement of the group of Africans who eventually became known as African-Americans has become even more significant, in view of the apparent perpetual prevalence of anti-African racism here in the United States. Professor Okolo poignantly notes that while most societies, in their onward march from hunter-gatherer evolutionary primitivity into a civilized and sedentary regime, logically transcended the hitherto predatory and bestial culture of slavery, in the case of continental Africa, such organic and salutary transformation was brutally and summarily interrupted by the advent of the Western industrial revolution. Consequently, by implication, the terms and the course of the infamous Trans-Atlantic Slave Trade was almost unilaterally determined by the Western European initiators of the latter economic enterprise who also owned and operated most of the plantations in the so-called New World, between the Fifteenth and Nineteenth centuries. For Professor Okolo, therefore, it is squarely within such historiographical and ideological parameters in which the massive and brutal enslavement of continental Africans in the foregoing period must be envisaged.

For the preceding reasons, this Nigerian critic of **Wonders of the African World** strongly questions the historical validity and accuracy of Ghanaian historian Dr. Akosua Perbi's rather curious assertion that: "There would have been no slave trade in the [African] countries [or regions which served as major markets for the commercial exportation of African humanity] without the complicity and [willful] collaboration of the [African] kings and their representatives." The critic acutely factors in the remarkable military disequilibrium—or political imbalance—between Europe and Africa on the eve of the Trans-Atlantic Trade in African humanity. To this effect, Professor Okolo notes: "After all, many of our leaders objected strongly to colonialism when the West decided on that, yet they were not able to stop such colonial onslaught."

In sum, Professor Okolo aptly suggests, any attempt to critically discuss the historical participation of continental African potentates in the enslavement of their own people abroad, must equally take account of the fact that for every African traditional ruler who collaborated with the European slavocrats, there were perhaps eight or nine others who were morally revolted by this heinous commercial regime and, in fact, fiercely fought to either prevent or promptly reverse such deleterious trend.

Needless to say, the preceding has always been the stance of this writer, contrary to what Professor Gates and his legions of cynical and misguided supporters would have the rest of the world believe. Thus, for instance, when the author-narrator of **Wonders of the African World** interviewed purported experts on the issue of African self-enslavement in the post-colonial republic of Benin and the Asante region of modern Ghana, Professor Henry Louis Gates, Jr., ought to have logically looked for other kingdoms, such as the Akyem-Abuakwa State of Ghana, whose leaders fiercely defended their people and themselves against the unmitigable assault of the imperialistic and slavocratic Asante. In fine, paint-brushing the entire West African sub-region as the unbested and unprecedented beehive of slave-mongering—or "Slave Kingdoms"—as the Harvard University humanities professor did, not only unpardonably insulted the intelligence of the people in the entire sub-region but, even more perniciously, it glibly falsified the fluxional realities of history. Professor Okolo also aptly echoes the late astute African-American historian Dr. John Henrik Clarke, who invariably emphasized the need for African and African-American Studies curricula to incorporate a comprehensive aspect of ancient and medieval European history in order for the student of global African studies to amply appreciate the global African experience over the last half-millennium. Professor Okolo further suggests the following quite constructive pedagogical approach to a study of the Trans-Atlantic Slave Trade: "To deal with that question, I usually get students to understand that Slavery did not originate in Africa or with blacks. The normal conception is that we have been culturally conditioned to associate the word 'slave' with blacks and Africa. Yet, linguistically, the word slave did not originally refer to blacks or Africa. It was derived from *slavs* who were historically subjected to unmitigated servitude after their migration to Europe from Asia from the 5th Century BC. Furthermore, apart from the historical use of *slavs* as slaves in Europe, slaves had been part of the historical realities of most societies as they progressed from the

'Hunting and Gathering' phase which was the most primitive [stage] of society known to man."

Perhaps Professor Gates would have done African historiographical scholarship and himself, as well as the rest of us, great good to have sought out the likes of Professors Okolo, Inikori and Gloria Emeagwali before embarking on his apparently oversized and overwhelming project which culminated in the filmic documentary titled **Wonders of the African World**. And to be surprisingly certain, there are many more articulate and erudite students and scholars of African Studies and Culture right here in the United States than on the entire African continent, largely due to socioeconomic and political factors. And almost certainly, most of these scholars and experts would have gladly volunteered assistance to Professor Gates if he had demonstrated humility and sincerity for such critical input. Unfortunately, the disciplinarily ubiquitous Skip Gates appears to have mistaken the professional validation accorded him by the imperious dons at Harvard University as a licential carte blanche to fabricate his own version of global African history. The foregoing appears to have largely informed the fact that Skip Gates elected to interview Dr. Oheneba Poku, son of the late Asantehene, or King Opoku-Ware II. Here, the one grievous misjudgment committed by the Oxbridge alumnus was to readily equate the son or dauphin of a patriarchal Western monarchy with that of a matrilineal Akan, traditional African society. For unlike a patriarchal society where the son of a king is a prince, among the Akan of Ghana, the Ivory Coast and elsewhere, the son or daughter of a reigning king is just an "Oheneba," a son or daughter of the King. The Akan coordinate—or equivalent—of an European "Prince" is "Ohenewofaase" or "Ohenewofaasewaa," in the case of a woman; and the two preceding cases translate, respectively, as "King's Nephew" and "King's Niece." Among the Akan, it is the distaff nephews and nieces of the reigning king who are the heirs apparent to the monarchy. The sons and daughters of kings belong to their mothers' families, except in formerly quite common cases of monarchical endogamy, whereby for purely political purposes, rather than such capricious whims as beauty and love, or romance, for that matter, an **Ohenewofaase** (or heir apparent) was prevailed upon to marry his maternal uncle's daughter. It was, indeed, the abject failure of Skip Gates to fully appreciate this critical aspect of Akan culture that prompted him to commit the blunder of interviewing the son of the late Asante King (Opoku Ware II) on the equally critical question of the Asante nation's participation in the Trans-Atlantic Slave Trade. Had he humbled himself as he ought to, Skip Gates would have instead asked to be shown the Chief Linguist—or royal spokesman—who also doubles as the traditional historian. And even though most of these linguists tend not to be highly schooled in Western institutional terms, they often are privy to much more information or knowledge than the average Western-educated African with a doctoral degree. Professor Gates obviously did not know or understand this rudimentary fact, which was why he sat on camera, with a fatuously long face, lamenting the otiose fact that Dr. Oheneba Poku, who holds a doctoral degree in Business Administration from Duke University, here in the United States, did not qualify to mount or ascend his late father's throne. What makes Gates' quizzical expression of regret even more fatuous stems from his hasty conclusion or dialectical presumption that other than Dr. Oheneba Poku, perhaps no other male personality at Manhyia, the Asante royal palace, or stool-house, was as well-educated or monarchically qualified as the Gatesian candidate. Indeed, it is on this score that one cannot but completely concur with Professor Mazrui's epithet of BLACK ORIENTALISM, in describing Skip Gates' apparently pathological disdain for traditional African institutions and culture. But here also, it is significant to assert our vehement disagreement with Professor Mazrui on the blatantly barbarous practice of Female Genital Mutilation (FGM) or excision. And on this score, we must hasten to emphasize that while the practice is widespread and prevalent on the African continent, not all major African cultures indulge or even encourage such practice, a salient example of which is the Akan multi-nation.

Using a Diopian approach to critical appreciation of the Trans-Atlantic Slave Trade, Professor Joseph Inikori observes that the two most significant factors which facilitated the massive African enslavement by Western Europeans between the mid-Fifteenth and mid-Nineteenth centuries were: (1) The existence of markets for slaves—on the African continent—as well as highly developed transportation systems that facilitated a relatively easy access and supply to these markets; and (2) The existence of weakly organized communities—or nations—whose members could be [readily] captured and sold at the barest minimum of risk or danger to the captors. The critic notes that it took the Norman conquest of 1066 to stanch the slave trade in the British Isles, just as it would take the Ottoman Turks and the Persians to liberate the Slavs in most of Eastern and Central Europe, as well as the Black Sea region. In Africa, such salutary political contingency was brutally preempted by the Spanish invasion of the so-called Western Sudan, post-colonial West Africa, which resulted in the fragmentation and destabilization of the region. On the preceding score, Professor Inikori observes: "The switch [in] demand from products [natural and mineral resources] to [human] captives occurred at a time when the vast majority of African communities on the Atlantic coast and the hinterlands were politically fragmented.

For example, in the small area of the Gold Coast (the coast of contemporary Ghana), with a population of no more than [one] hundred thousand in the 17th century, there were about 43 autonomous chiefdoms at this time. Given this fragmentation, there were few governments strong enough to prevent internal breach of law and order in the face of large-scale European demand for captives, let alone prevent external aggressors from taking captives."

It is quite regrettable, however, that Professor Inikori fails to further advance his otherwise brilliant argument by merely hinting at the fact that between the late Seventeenth and Nineteenth centuries, when the Trans-Atlantic Slave Trade reached its apogee—or apex—many of the most powerful European slave traders moved their headquarters to Lagos, the colonial and early post-colonial capital of Nigeria. In fact, the entire region of Southern Nigeria and the Bight of Benin became known as the "Slave Coast," for nearly half of all West Africans deported for free labor in the so-called New World came from the "Slave Coast." Surprisingly and interestingly, most of the Nigerian scholars who participated in the debate that swirled around Professor Gates' *Wonders of the African World*, virtually ignored this salient reality. And so one comes away from the massive intellectual fare on this subject, as accessed via the Internet, feeling a wistfully debilitating sense of disappointment. That only a piddling few of these scholars impugn Skip Gates' rather flimsy pretext for not filming a portion of his "wondrous" documentary on the "Slave Kingdoms," is to be unreservedly deplored. It is, however, Trinidadian scholar Gloria Emeagwali, a longtime resident of post-colonial Nigeria, who delivers the most poignant and critically astute blow. The State University of Connecticut professor notes that the Trans-Atlantic Slave Trade involved a critical component of transfer technology, with such "physical trappings of enslavement, including shackles, branding, Euro-Christianity…as well as [the] increasingly racist notions of the 'Other,' very much determining the contours and extent of African enslavement."

28

Unlike many of us who criticized Skip Gates for the hatchet work that is his filmic documentary **Wonders of the African World**, it just could be that what repulses Professor Mazrui is that Skip Gates embarks on precisely the same agenda which Mazrui pursued in his 1986 documentary titled **The Africans: A Triple Heritage**. In the latter documentary, Mazrui pursues an ideology labeled **AFRABIA**, whereby indigenous or so-called Black Africans and North African Arabs are perceived to be unsuspecting **Twin-Victims** of European imperialism. The basis for Mazrui's ideology is that North African Arabs and indigenous Africans share the same continent. Furthermore, the Organization of African Unity (OAU), which theoretically morphed into an entity called the African Union (AU), has a membership composed of both indigenous Africans and Arabs.

Here, what Mazrui woefully fails to address is the fact that it took almost the single-handed and single-minded initiative of Ghanaian president Dr. Kwame Nkrumah, with the indefatigable and missionary assistance of such Diasporic Africans as Dr. W. E. B. DuBois and Mr. George Padmore (a.k.a. Malcolm Nurse), of the United States and Trinidad, respectively, to bring about the establishment of the OAU. The powerful and inspirational writings of Jamaica's Marcus Mosiah Garvey also played no small part in the intellectual formation and development of President Nkrumah; there were also a legion others too numerous to enumerate or recall. And it is hardly hyperbolical to observe that the geopolitical and nominal acceptance by many a North African leader of his Africanity was largely the brainchild of President Nkrumah. And to date, most North Africans, at best, maintain a polite and tentative rapport with indigenous Africans. And the erudite Professor Mazrui cannot deny an awareness of this bizarre fact.

Unfortunately, the renowned Kenyan political scientist's attempt to plead the cause of Arabia—or the Arab world—by making the latter a twin-victim with indigenous Africans has, so far, not washed. One salient reason for this is that the historical presence of North African Arabs is as violent as the attendant factors and events subtending the massive enslavement and psychical annihilation of Africans by Western Europeans between the Fifteenth and Nineteenth centuries. Indeed, Professor Mazrui, in his filmic documentary titled **The Africans: A Tri-**

ple Heritage tactfully plays fast and loose, as it were, with the collective memory of indigenous Africans. He actually mentions the fact that Islam, and by tacit implication Arabs, have resided on the African continent for some twelve centuries (or 1,200 years), almost as if such temporal longevity in of itself excuses Arabo-African atrocities in such perennially troubled spots as Mauritania and Sudan. Instead, the Afro-Arab narrator of *The Africans* sneeringly downplays the enormity of indigenous African enslavement for most of the pre-medieval era, by rather irresponsibly and disingenuously comparing the current numbers of citizens in the Arab world who trace their descent to the African continent. Either wittingly or unwittingly, Dr. Mazrui fails to note the fact that equally or, perhaps, even greater numbers of African descended people as reside in the Arab world today were also sold to Europeans by these same Arabs; and as it is to be naturally expected, as many Africans as were able to assimilate into Arab societies also may certainly be expected to have been assimilated by the European societies into which these indigenous Africans were exported or deported.

Another factor which Professor Mazrui fails to account for is that the more anterior—or ancient—enslavement of Africans by Arabs contributed immensely to the diachronic degradation of the African personality throughout much of the world outside the African continent. That the problem of race is perhaps even more acute when it comes to assessing the relationship between indigenous Africans and North African Arabs, is glaringly evinced by an Egyptian segment of Professor Mazrui's filmic documentary titled *The Africans: A Triple Heritage*. The issue regards the salient factors underlying the Islamic fundamentalist assassination of President Anwar el-Sadat in the early 1980s. In his documentary, Professor Mazrui subtly papers over the lethal question of race—more precisely "Blackness"—in post-colonial Egyptian society. Consequently, the leading Kenyan political scientist almost glibly concludes that President Sadat was simply executed by his own soldiers because the slain peacemaker had blundered by extending the proverbial olive branch to the late Israeli Prime Minister Menachem Begin. Interestingly, as Hisham Aidi, a writer whose name points to his Arabo-Islamic background poignantly observed in an article titled "'Libyans Are Africans': Race and Identity in North Africa" (Africana.com 11/2/00), "The issue of racial identification has long been a contentious topic in Egypt. In 1984, Columbia Pictures launched a television series on the life of the then recently assassinated Egyptian president Anwar Sadat, which starred Louis Gossett, Jr. When the series was banned in Egypt, many speculated that the production had offended political and religious sensibilities, but *New York Times* journalist Judith Miller cited racial reasons. 'Throughout his presidency, Mr. Sadat appeared particularly sensitive about his dark complexion, which prompted jokes and ridicule,' she wrote. 'The portrayal of Mr. Sadat as a black man has revived the issue of race in Egypt, where it is usually deeply submerged.' Because of Egyptians' discomfort with Sadat's representation as a black man, Miller argues, national authorities chose to ban the film rather than confront the unsettling issues it raised."

Needless to say, the dastardly attempts by the Egyptian government to discursively and culturally proscribe the subject of race is rather infantile, and one that is not likely to go away for as long as Egypt and the rest of the African continent exist. But it is also significant to note that one of President Sadat's parents was widely known to have been a Nubian from southern Egypt, around the area where the world-famous Aswan Dam is located. And what is even more significant, Mr. Sadat was known to have publicly acknowledged his indigenous Africanity. Thus his alleged sensitivity about his blackness, obviously had more to do with the ungodly treatment accorded indigenous Africans by official Egypt. And this is hardly surprising, since most of the current leaders of Egypt, including Mr. Hosni Mubarak, are descendants of Turkish slaves, known historically as the Mamelukes, who controlled Egyptian politics between 1250 and 1517, and have continued to significantly influence political and cultural institutions until now. And as the great Senegalese scholar Cheikh Anta Diop scientifically testified, nearly 70-percent of the ancient Egyptian pharaohs were indigenous Africans, not Afro-Arabs or any such genetic and cultural hybrids. It is also quite interesting that modern Jews also claim kinship with the pharaoh Ramses II. About ten years ago, the **New York Times** published an editorial celebrating the purported discovery of the tomb of this great African monarch, thereby supposedly authenticating the ancient Egyptian heritage of modern Jews. Some of us, back then, envisaged the entire matter with great amusement, particularly when many American-Jews joined in the celebration, knowing for ourselves that most American-Jews are of European descent and are not known to claim any genetic filiation or affinity with either continental Africans or African-Americans. Of course, we also knew that those Jews who claimed descent from Pharaoh Ramses II were not totally without historical evidence. For not only had the originally Iraqi-Jews not spent nearly a half-millennium in Egypt, both as tyrants and slaves, but even one of the wives of their patriarch, Moses, a prince of the Egyptian court, was an indigenous African from the modern-day country of the Sudan. And so when the former director of the Cultural Office of the Egyptian Embassy in Washington, D. C., Mr. Abdel-Latif Abou-Ela wrote his vociferous protestation titled "Egypt Says Ramses II Wasn't Black," those of us who knew better were not fazed. This is because when all is said and done, the ancient Egyptians were not the progenitors or ancestors of the Arabs of modern Egypt, most of whose literate populace does not even read the ancient Egyptian script, the way modern Hebrews are able to read some of the ancient Hebraic scripts. And it is also significant to note that there are legions of indigenous African scholars and linguists hard at work attempting to scientifically link the language and culture of ancient Egypt to the indigenous cultures of the rest of the African continent. To date, among the prime candidates of ancient Egyptian heritage are the Akan of Ghana, the Ivory Coast and other parts of the African continent, as well as, of course, the Diaspora.

And talking of genetic and cultural filiations, not very long ago, I read in the **New York Times** about the president of the Comoros Islands who, by the way, happens to have an Akan name. He is called President Assoumani, an obvious variation on the traditional Ghanaian Asomaning, or Asomani, an Akan of possible Akwamu extraction. The Akwamu are one of the original Akan nation-builders of modern Ghana. Like the Asante, their successors, the Akwamu fiercely battled the Dutch and the Danes in the era of the Trans-Atlantic Slave Trade; and it is not quite improbable that President Assoumani's ancestors were among the great resistance fighters who were exiled for standing up to Western slavo-colonial degradation. In any case, it clearly appears to this writer that the raging ideological animosity between Nigerian Nobel playwright laureate Professor Wole Soyinka and Dr. Ali A. Mazrui, firmly hinges on the latter's apparent lack of chutzpah in frontally tackling the unflattering Afro-Arab historiographical icon in the collective indigenous African imagination. This issue would be further examined in the next segment of our series.

29

As we bring this series to an inevitable conclusion, it becomes necessary to tie up the proverbial loose-ends. And while I have been aware of the many readers of this column, I have not had the kind of feedback that would enable me to gauge more objectively the disparate and diverse responses of my readers. Most of the awareness regarding my audience has come in the form of an interjection or two at such public places as supermarkets and social gatherings. Some have also called to congratulate me on such bold initiative and to wish me "more grease to your elbows." In all such situations and circumstances, I have not hesitated to point out that this undertaking has been singularly predicated on the imperative need for posterity—both in the Diaspora and on the African continent—to be bequeathed an indispensable legacy of truth and forthrightness—and I have always deemed these to be the least that our generation can hope to bequeath, short of making the material existence of posterity much, much better than we have been blessed with in our time.

But, perhaps, even more significantly, embarking on this journey has brought my attention to the great need for such public-friendly intellectual discourse regarding the place of global Africans, as well as the primeval continent, in general, in global historiographical epistemology. For it was wisely observed long ago that when lies—even well-intentioned lies—are allowed to be produced and disseminated unchallenged, sooner than later, such mendacity may come to be identified with the truth, and the consequences are often deadly at a multiplicity of levels. The perpetration and perpetuation of most crimes against humanity are often predicated upon the woeful acceptance of abject mendacity as a substitute for scientific objectivity. In Europe, such wretched state of historiography resulted in the massive enslavement and extermination of Jews and that often-ignored nationality of humans called Roma, or Gypsies. And to be certain, the equally untold experiences of the Roma in the context of the Nazi Holocaust has yet to be fully retailed. And the reason for such default is largely political, for the production and dissemination of knowledge—for good and ill—is invariably determined by one's collective power as a group to manufacture one's own brand of reality and prompt others to believe and treat it as such. And the relative lack of power on the part of global Africans has logically implied that non-Africans would produce and disseminate our story, often with the callous and thoughtless complicity of some among our own, thus deviously but deftly giving credence to what might otherwise be deemed to be patently and unpardonably outrageous and outright offensive.

Among the most memorable feedback received during the course of our series is one that came from Mr. Eddie Hampton, Jr., of Brooklyn, New York. We hereby reproduce Mr. Hampton's letter in its entirety: "Dear Prof. Kwame Oko-ampa-Ahoofe, Jr.: I have read your article entitled 'The New Scapegoats—Part Twenty-One,' in *The New York Beacon* dated: December 16-December 22, 2004./I think it is pathetic that articles such as yours criticizing Mr. Henry Louis Gates' work are in effect proving his point; Africans are still selling Africans./Here you are attacking a Black man in public with the intent of discrediting his work. It would seem to me that the proper way to influence Mr. Gates would be to write to him personally, or perhaps do a comparative work that debunks his the-ory./While I am not a scholar or a historian [,] I found Mr. Gates' work [to be] very informative and unique[,] considering [that] no one else has done something on the level and with [the kind of] sophistication that he has. I am convinced that anyone trying to do research on such level as Mr. Gates will [sic] probably make some mistakes [;] however[,] I don't think that we should 'throw the baby out with the bath-water.'/What I have seen is that very often we may have the best intent in mind [sic], as I suspect that you have[;] however, we are often our own worst enemy./Sincerely,/Eddie Hampton Jr."

The following is an exact reproduction of my original E-mail response to the preceding: "Dear Mr. Hampton:/Thank you for reading and promptly respond-ing to my article ('The New Scapegoats—Part Twenty-One,' *The New York Beacon* 12/16-22/04). Unfortunately, I could not disagree with you more vehe-mently that Dr. Henry Louis Gates, Jr's 'Wonders of the African World' is highly informative./Actually, the aforementioned documentary does quite the opposite of either informing or educating its viewers; and, by the way, I have also read the accompanying textbook of the film which is even more damning and mischie-vous than the latter. In fine, what Professor Gates achieves is simply deprecating and demonizing continental Africans; and I believe I ought to know this, because I am a continental African with a specialty in global African history and culture./And if you really desire to know more about continental Africans, then you need to see British historian Basil Davidson's pioneering documentary titled 'Africa: The Story of a Continent' [1984]. To be certain, it was the preceding documen-tary upon which both Kenyan scholar Ali A. Mazrui—author of 'The Africans: A Triple Heritage'—and Professor Henry Louis Gates based their respective documentaries. There are also quite a number of authoritative monographs on two-thousand-plus years of African history./Indeed, while Dr. Gates has every right to portray continental Africans in any light that he deems appropriate, it is also significant to observe that he is no pioneer in the discipline of African history. The man is, self-confessedly, not even a historian! What, indeed, makes his work seem to be pioneering largely stems from the fact that there is a woeful lack of any substantive historiographical appreciation of Africa here in the United States, generally speaking./No, I did not deem it appropriate to write personally to Professor Gates after the fact. Indeed, had he [critically] considered the humanity of continental Africans as worthwhile, the man would not have told the president of PBS-TV, in the wake of the broadcasting of his documentary, that at best he, Dr. Gates, considered the continental African to be 'my distant relative.'/Once again, thank you very much for your letter; my very best wishes!/Sincerely,/Kwame Okoampa-Ahoofe, Jr., Ph.D."

Indeed, while I found Mr. Hampton's letter to be quite commendable for its bold exposition of the reader's grievances, I also found it to be typically condescending, particularly where the writer makes the following observation: "What I have seen is that very often we may have the best intent in mind, as I suspect that you have[;] however, we are often our own worst enemy." In essence, the argument of the writer is that perhaps I was a little under the weather or intoxicated with whatever the imaginative reader could fathom to be able to effectively understand, much less, articulate my concerns vis-à-vis Professor Gates' **Wonders of the African World**. That I could hardly be serious in my observations. Of course, one clearly garners the latter impression when one reads the following paragraph from Mr. Hampton's letter: "While I am not a scholar or a historian[,] I found Mr. Gates' work [to be] very informative and unique[,] considering [that] no one else has done something on the level and with [the kind of] sophistication that he has. I am convinced that anyone trying to do research on such level as Mr. Gates will [sic] probably make some mistakes[;] however, I don't think that we should 'throw the baby out with the bath-water'."

Indeed, what makes the foregoing quote from Mr. Hampton rather quaint and humorous is that one cannot be certain just "whose baby" the writer has in mind, whom we risk throwing out with the bath-water. And don't get me wrong, I speak Akan-Twi with a respectable modicum of command and so proverbs and maxims are pretty pedestrian to me. But here, needless to say, we are more interested in reiterating the premise with which we began this segment of our series: The commonplace observation that when lies and falsehoods are allowed to go unchallenged, sooner than later, they come to be reckoned as epistemic gems. For how does Mr. Hampton come by his rather immodest presumption that "no one else has done something on the level and with [the] sophistication that he [Skip Gates] has," unless either Mr. Gates himself or his sponsors wittingly or unwittingly gave the writer such erroneous impression? We are also intrigued by Mr. Hampton's quite frontal and logical riposte that: "It would seem to me that the proper way to influence Mr. Gates would be to write to him personally, or perhaps do a comparative work that debunks his theory."

First of all, it has never been the intention of this series and its author to influence Mr. Gates in any way, shape or form, whatsoever. Our primary interest has been and continues to be about setting the records straight, as it were. And on this score, it is apt to emphatically observe that Skip Gates has no especial preserve on the epistemological content and dissemination of global African history, any more or less than any other student, scholar or intellectual in the discipline of global African history and culture. And so to try to influence the Harvard University director of African-American Studies would be woefully limiting and uninstructive. Neither is it our intent in this series to merely seek to "discredit" Skip Gates' humongous corpus of multi-media production on global African Studies. And here, also, we must hasten to add that while, like many of his ilk, Gatesian scholarship adds a welcome dimension to global African scholarship, in general, it is neither unique nor indispensable, any more than this author's creative and scholarly output is. Indeed, the stolid era of personality cults, both political and intellectual, is far behind our time. Nonetheless, as we observed earlier, the curious and intellectually critical likes of Mr. Hampton make our work worthwhile, in the sense that such critical thinkers constantly hold our feet to the fire, as it were, and inspire us to doggedly ferret out the truth as we diligently go about our multi-disciplinary activities as Afrocentric scholars, students, artists, authors and consumers of global African scholarship and culture.

Another significant dimension of global African scholarship that needs to be seriously discussed is the perennial question of **Africanity** or **African Identity**. For the question of who and what constitutes an African has become even more significant in the post-colonial era, with particular reference to the indeflectible reality of the massive, historical occupation of the North African region by ethnic Arabs. Not only has such a discussion become imperative vis-à-vis the raging interracial dilemma in Sudan's Darfur and Southern regions, where the Arab-dominated military regime of President Mohammed Omar Al-Bashir has virtually reduced indigenous Sudanese to indigent refugee status but, even more importantly, one's ability, or lack thereof, to determine one's identity is inextricably interlinked with one's existential viability among the comity of nations.

Indeed, the European slavers of Africans very much appreciated this fact more than most of their enemies and neighbors, which was why the discrete identities of Africans in the Diaspora had to be cannibalized, particularly with regard to the retention of African languages and cultures.

In his mordant critique of Skip Gates' **Wonders of the African World**, Professor Mazrui raises the question of Afro-Arab identity in a quite disturbing way; and it is disturbing because the highly respectable Kenyan scholar appears to woefully underestimate the blisteringly perennial impact of ethnic and cultural alienation on the political stability and collective development of continental Africa. On this score, in his "Millennium [sic] Letter to Henry Louis Gates, Jr.: Concluding a Dialogue," the leading East African political scientist observes: "There is a logical fallacy [that] you commit more than once in the TV series. You claim [that] Zanzibari claiming to be Arab or Persian is like you claiming to be WHITE! The analogy is totally false. It is like you claiming to be IRISH, White. If one of your grandparents was Irish, there are societies which would permit you to be [identified as] Irish. [Unfortunately] it happens that mainstream America does not permit you to identify yourself with your Irish ancestor. That is a decision made by mainstream America and not by you. The lineage system in Zanzibar, on the other hand, does permit people to continue to be [identified as] Arab or Persian generations after their Arab or Persian **great** forebear [immigrant/settler on the African continent has passed on]. Why did you choose to interview simple people in Zanzibar who claim to be Persians? Did you want to embarrass them before cameras by their apparent lack of sophistication?"

In fact, the preceding abstract may yet be the proverbial **Rosetta Stone** that holds the key to a scientific, or objective, appreciation for the Janus-faced temperaments of Professors Mazrui and Gates. For as our series winds to a close, it is intriguingly becoming apparent that Professor Ali A. Mazrui and Dr. Henry Louis Gates, Jr., are two faces of the same post-colonial, global African identity crisis. The couple could even be aptly regarded as twin-brothers, of course, assuming one were wont to discounting the barely half-generation of temporal distance between them. For the seventeen-year difference between Professor Mazrui and Skip Gates either makes the former the elder sibling of the latter, or the latter, the elder nephew of the former. This inverse formula is intriguingly plausible because it very much mirrors this writer's own relationship with his youngest maternal uncle, Lt.-Col. (Ret.) Leslie Edward Sintim, of the Ghana Armed Forces. And such relationship can be quite irritating sometimes, because it is that kind of between and betwixt relationship in which that which is often appears to be more of that which seems. Thus when the Kenyan scholar calls himself "The Africanist Elder" of his younger African-American counterpart, the latter is apt to mentally gauge the temporal stature of his own parents and promptly retort: "No way, Ali!" and gruffly add under his smoking breath: "You are just ten years older than my elder brother."

Indeed, when Professor Mazrui accuses Skip Gates of taking advantage of "simple [or lowly-educated] Zanzibari who claim to be Persian," we couldn't disagree with the Kenyan political scientist more vehemently; for it is precisely the simple people, rather than the highly sophisticated and deviously hypocritical, who accurately serve as veritable weather vanes by which to measure the extent of the socio-cultural alienation of these hybrid Africans. For almost nowhere in the rest of the so-called Black Africa, would any of the least educated, even those with known **great** European missionary and colonial forebears vociferously insist on being recognized as Dutch, English or Portuguese, long after their ancestors have descended into virtual oblivion. And the fact that most of the "simple people in Zanzibar" whom Skip Gates interviewed claimed Arabo-Persian heritage, even when they no longer spoke Arabic and Persian, pretty much reflects the caustic inferiority complex which afflicts them. And rather than fuming at Skip Gates for supposedly making fools of these lost tribes of Africans, Professor Mazrui ought to be about the salutary business of educating his "own Swahili" kinsfolk. And this is likely to be a difficult task, particularly since Professor Mazrui appears himself to have made a similar choice earlier in his life. Elsewhere, the Kenyan political scientist observes that some prominent members of his agnatic family changed their cognomen of "Mazrui," which is Omani-Arab, into something more African, in order to shear themselves of the family's slavocratic past.

Professor Mazrui, on the other hand, had decided to straddle two horses by retaining the **great** Mazrui name. But what is even more disturbing about his choice of identity is Professor Mazrui's implicit claim that continental African societies, somehow, allow some of their members to disdainfully assume Arabo-Persian-o—foreign—identities, for the hardly productive reason that some forgotten **great** ancestor was of Arabic or Persian descent. It may, indeed, be this elusive and protean aspect of the **Mazruian** political and cultural ideology which Professor Wole Soyinka decries when the equally great Nigerian scholar and playwright accuses Professor Mazrui of hypocritically harboring a "halfway-house" attitude towards his African identity.

30

It has been a pretty long, exacting and occasionally tedious but, over all, a worthwhile trip. The objective, as those of you who have faithfully and studiously trav-
eled along with us might aptly attest, was not to silence or muffle the seemingly
intractable and insuperable debate on the Trans-Atlantic Slave Trade. Were the
preceding the case, our journey would have amounted to nothing short of the
Quixotic. Rather, we aimed to render this perennial dilemma a little more discursively cognitive, historical and constructive than desultorily emotional and
recriminatory, as the Harvard school of Africanists, spearheaded by Dr. Henry
Louis Gates, Jr., sought to make it. That the Gatesian school of continental African incrimination woefully failed in its efforts, some $10 million-plus and digi-
tized, state-of-the-art technology later, is clearly borne out by the following
historiographically objective observation by Dr. Ibrahim K. Sundiata, chairman
of the Department of History at Howard University. "Most societies have had
some form of it. Slavery, at best, rests on the [capacity] to coerce labor and/or sex-
ual reproduction. Probing for a peculiar 'Black' guilt for slavery is an ahistorical
and presentist [i.e. anachronistic?] trap. We might as well ask why the 'brothers'
have fought and killed each other in places as disparate as Biafra and Rwanda.
The answer is obvious. Africa is a continent full of proud, diverse and often contentious peoples. It also has social cleavages within societies, something a scholar
like Walter Rodney clearly recognized twenty years ago. Joe Miller has pointed
out that: 'Africa [still] looms integrally in the background of African-American
history as a unified ancestry reflecting the racial sense of community forced by
[White-America] on African Americans....' **Wonders of the African World** did
little to go beyond this [unhistorical] view. The positing of a Black 'Volksgemein-
schaft' is soothingly mythopoeic, but not history. As Pearle-Alice
Marsh…laments: 'There are millions of Americans who still think Africa is a
country, not a continent.' Sadly, in spite of its kaleidoscopic race around the continent, **Wonders of the African World** will do little to change this perception."

Indeed, had Skip Gates spent a little time reading President Kwame Nkrumah's ideological classic titled **Consciencism**, he would have intelligently mastered the vertical intricacies of traditional African societies, thereby saving himself
the utter embarrassment of treating continental Africans as a monolithic entity.

His academic year's sojourn in Tanzania during the early 1970s ought to have apprised the Harvard humanities professor of this basic fact; and he would also have clearly understood that while most African societies are not industrialized, and therefore relatively materially identical, in terms of political and cultural levels of advancement, these countries are diverse as any in other regions of the world. For example, while China, India, Korea—both North and South—and Japan are all Asian countries, they could not be objectively characterized as collectively homogeneous merely because they are all populated by Asiatic phenotypes. Professor Sundiata is also apt in highlighting the fact that raging hostilities among Africans within the same geopolitical confines, even in the post-colonial era, ought to have enlightened his Cambridge, Massachusetts, colleague of the fluxional complexities of Africanity. But those of us who have been studiously following the flamboyant, public career of Skip Gates firmly understand why he blundered so mercilessly with his **Wonders of the African World**, both the film and the text accompanying the latter. Earlier on, while he was being sweetly courted by White-America and being made to feel **sui generis**—a class act all by himself—the Piedmont, West Virginian native determined that any Afrocentric scholar who was not being equally courted by the proverbial White-Master was, perforce, a thoroughgoing charlatan. Thus, Dr. Kwame Nkrumah is not wont to have met the Gatesian criteria for a scholar worthy of critical attention. He, in all likelihood, must have branded the modern Ghanaian patriarch a leftist radical too full of passion and woefully short on reason. And he would most likely have had the staunch support of Professor Anthony Kwame Appiah, whose inveterate animosity for President Nkrumah appears to largely stem from the incarceration of the elder Mr. Joe Appiah by the immortalized Ghanaian premier. Indeed, in the encyclopedia which Skip Gates co-edited with the younger Mr. Appiah, the latter has little that is edifying to say about the founder of modern Ghana. Appiah, in his entry, has President Nkrumah dying in exile in Guinea, instead of Romania. Nkrumah had, of course, lived most of his years of exile in President Ahmed Sekou Toure's Guinea, but he had not died in the latter country. It is also quite certain that even if he had read the path-paving works of Afro-Guyanese historian and thinker Dr. Walter Rodney, Skip Gates would have promptly dismissed them as hogwash or sheer polemic, as one of my graduate school professors had the occasion to do. For so embittered has Professor Gates become of Africa and her people that any attempt at portraying these primeval human beings in terms of their humanity is virtually tantamount to blasphemy. Africans, in the mythical and hallucinatory imagination of our MacArthur Foundation genius, could be deemed to be nothing short of unconscionable, criminal collaborators of European slavocrats.

Even so, we are glad to have had the opportunity to critically engage our self-hating "distant cousin." The sad, and perhaps paradoxically salutary, reality is that any chance for lasting conciliation with our distant cousin might well have been irreparably lost. Not that any of us harbor any grudge against our West Virginian "former kin," it is simply that he has ostracized himself from our global African family in a way that would make our ancestors look upon the British imperialist cormorant Cecil John Rhodes, with far greater sympathy. For at least this continental Africa's arch-nemesis was humble enough, during the twilight of his days, to have instructed his kin and minions to inter his remains among the very people whose humanity he had impugned and whose property he had callously expropriated.

Indeed, Professor Ibrahim Sundiata appreciates his immutable Africanity in a way that Skip Gates might never be able to grasp. And the former does not strain to establish such historical reality. The very title of his rejoinder to his Harvard colleague more than eloquently speaks for itself: "ALL BROTHERS AND SISTERS, ALL THE TIME."

But it is Gwendolyn Mikell who more than eloquently calls Gatesian scholarship to proper account. In her rejoinder titled "Deconstructing Gates' 'Wonders of the African World,'" Ms. Mikell laments: "Unfortunately, it now appears to me that we have been sold a bill of [damaged] goods. We have been betrayed! Despite wonderful photography and rich visual images of Africa presented in the film, we have been let down. It appears to me that the content of the video built up and glorified Africa on the one hand, and denigrated it by [the] flinging of mud on the other hand. It seems to me that Gates' pain about the Trans-Atlantic Slave Trade had twisted his objectives as filmmaker and narrator. We all understand [the] pain and suffering related to slavery, but it is not acceptable to present negative personal attacks as historical opinions, [almost] as if they are fact in material that pretends to be scholarly. It seems to me that Gates has crafted his own attack on Afrocentric views of the greatness of Africa. It seems to me that the Gates video attempts to paint a picture of an imaginary division between African Americans and African views of the continent and its role in history. As an African American, this offends me and many others among my colleagues greatly."

Professor Mikell, it is both significant and edifying to observe, does not stop short of the preceding heart-rending plaintive. As a much more mature and cultured, Afrocentric scholar, the critic shrewdly cautions: "An Elder does not break wind in public, but in a latrine." She promptly reminds Skip Gates that the preceding quote is a traditional African proverb. But, here again, it is not clear whether having impudently defecated in the market square, and thus on the pates and faces of our African ancestors, Skip Gates has any modicum of appreciation for proverbs, which may be too idiomatic and recondite for the man, or that he even cares about the patently and, perhaps, injurious implications of his hatchet work on the primeval continent of his "distant relatives." Either way, at least we are elatedly rest-assured that a more thoughtful figure among his own has mastered the desired and necessary courage to call this wayward brat to order. Even so, in her unmistakably poignant lament, Professor Mikell is charitable enough to concede his imperious Cambridge colleague a modicum of intellectual decency, thus this observation: "It seems to me that Gates' pain about the Trans-Atlantic Slave Trade has twisted his objectives as [a] filmmaker and [a] narrator."

Indeed, Gates had no other known objectives other than the "twisted" mythology that he exuberantly provides readers and spectators in his *Wonders of the African World*. Fortunately for us, Professor Mikell is not in the least hoodwinked; for she acutely recognizes this unvarnished Gatesian objective for what it patently is: "Negative personal attacks [that are glibly passed off as] historical opinions [that in turn, brazenly] pretend to be scholarly." In sum, Ms. Mikell seems to intimate, so presumptuously self-assured has Professor Gates become as to facilely presume the bulk of his audience for clinical idiots such that he woefully failed to conduct even the barest minimum of historical research prior to undertaking his epic project. Consequently, in agreeing to sponsor his so-called *Wonders of the African World*, both the British Broadcasting Corporation (BBC-TV) and the Public Broadcasting System (PBS-TV) had indiscreetly assumed the unenviable role of a biased instructor dishing out "A" grades to the least prepared student in her/his class. And for good measure, Ms. Mikell further notes: "By failing to engage Africanist scholars as commentators (anthropologists, historians, political scientists, theologians, etc.), Gates allows his film to convey historically inaccurate inferences. He left the impression that the bulk of the slaves who made the middle passage came out of the Gold Coast and the Whydah area because of the [role of] the Ashanti and Dahomey kings, which is far from historically accurate. Those of us who have read Joseph Holloway's *Africanisms in American Culture*, or John Thornton's *Africa and Africans in the Making of the Atlantic World*, or Joseph Miller's *Ways of Death*, know that the reality is far more complex and varied. Slaves from the Guinea Coast of Senegambia, the rice coast of Sierra Leone, the Rivers areas of Nigeria, and more importantly, from the Congo-Angolan coasts, formed an enormous portion of the total numbers that made the middle passage to the Americas. Many were stolen by Western slave-traders and separated from families and communities, leaving these societies poorer than before. So where does Gates get his unique histories and interpretations of the Transatlantic Slave Trade that appear to address his own psychological conception of slavery?"

For his part Biko Agozino, who introduces himself as a South African, registers his acute disappointment at the Gatesian "Wonders." He also questions why the filmic documentary was broadcast by the BBC over the course of some six weeks but was broadcast by PBS over the span of an intensive three days. In sum, notes Mr. Agozino, by diffusing its broadcast of **Wonders** over six weeks, the BBC ended up courting relative disinterest among its audience. On the other hand, jam-packing its broadcast into a hectic three days ensured that PBS would court the sedulous attention of its audience, who could readily follow the sequence of events depicted. Even so, the South African critic expresses appreciable concern that as an educational resource, as intended by **Wonders'** author-narrator, the documentary was woefully inadequate, particularly because its ideological orientation was patently Eurocentric. "No educational text is ever without room for corrections and improvement or updating, hence the need for new editions every so often. In that connection, the curriculum should address a number of issues that the medium of television could not adequately capture in six hours, especially when the people behind the camera and those in charge of scripting and editing do not share the passion of the people watching the program without understandable trepidation."

And one such trepidation, according to Mr. Agozino, is the facile and pat manner in which Professor Gates depicted the historical African memory, particularly regarding the near-amnesiac manner in which the Harvard professor of African-American Literature portrayed the excruciating question of slavery in the post-colonial, continental African imagination: "As a descendant of Africans who survived the slave raids, I feel a close affinity with Professor Gates and all the African Americans who still suffer the psychological [trauma and] the slow-healing wounds of slavery. As a young boy, I remember going to live with my mother in her home village for a while. I was surprised to be informed that I [was not to] accept food in the compound of one of my maternal cousins because a person from that branch of the family [had] committed the abomination of selling a person from my mother's branch. The elders explained that such an abomination was not pardonable and the only way [of avoiding] disaster was by avoiding the ritual of breaking bread with the offender's branch of the family. The fact that this ritual breaking of the ties of blood is very rare in Africa is a direct evidence [of the fact that] it was very rare for Africans to sell their own kind into slavery"

("Wonders of the African Crisis" *West African Review* [2000] ISSN 1525-4488).

In Akan-Ghanaian traditional folklore, it is a known fact that before captives were sold into slavery, their totemic clan background was inquired into. And if the captive happened to share the same totem as his or her captor, the former was promptly offered protection. Hence, the maxim: "*Animguase Mfata Okan-niba*," which loosely translates as: "No person of Akan-ethnic descent deserves to be humiliated."

As we wind up this series, I also feel elated to share with readers a serendipitous discovery that I recently made regarding one of my paternal great-granduncles, King (Osagyefo) Amoako Atta I, paramount king of the Akyem(Achim)-Abuakwa State of Ghana and the Supreme Ruler of all the three Akyem states, including Kotoku and Bosome. Legend had it, while I was growing up that Osagyefo Amoako Atta I had been hostile to the spread of Christianity—specifically Basel or Presbyterian—education in his state because he was an illiterate sovereign who did not value the increasing significance of Western education. Well, recently I came across an essay titled "Amoako Atta and the British," written by Dr. Trevor R. Getz, of the University of New Orleans, that put an eloquent lie to the preceding claim. In his essay, Professor Getz notes that Nana Amoako Atta, who reportedly died of pneumonia on February 2, 1887, had actually been educated at the Kyebi (Kibi) Mission School, and had even "reputedly denied a request by an indigenous cleric to close the Christian school down." I proudly point out the preceding facts in order to underscore how a woeful lack of studious research could leave perennial historiographical distortions in the minds of readers. I also point this out because I was always of the damnable and erroneous impression that I was a fourth-generation in the line of the Western-educated members of my family. Now it turns out that I am actually among the fifth-generation; and there is no reason to doubt that further research might further extend this genealogical literacy table. Unfortunately, spatial strictures preclude detailing my latest finding. Suffice it to note, however, that long before the Asante King, Agyemang Prempeh I, was exiled by the British in the Seychelles in 1896, King Amoako-Atta I had been deported to Lagos, Nigeria (1880-85). His sole crime against the British was that the Osagyefo had mobilized forces aimed at dealing a lasting blow—a sort of Final Solution—to the bellicose and belligerent Asante who had been incessantly harassing the Akyem states. Had he been allowed to trounce the Asante, who at this time appeared to be on fairly friendly terms with the British, after the former's 1874 devastating defeat by the Akyem, in the pay of the British (i.e. Sir Garnet Worsley?) perhaps the geopolitical map between the two most powerful traditional, Ghanaian states would have been remarkably altered, and with it their respective national attitudes. This, of course, is a matter that we hope to take up in the near future. In any case, may we take this privileged opportunity to express our sincere gratitude to our faithful readers. LONG LIVE GLOBAL AFRICA!!!

ABOUT THE AUTHOR

The 1999 winner of the Best Essay Award by *Nassau Review*, for his controversial essay "When Human Dignity is Besieged: An Afrocentric Critique of the *Diary of Anne Frank*, Kwame Okoampa-Ahoofe, Jr., was born and raised in Ghana. In 1988, he was the first poet to receive the John J. Reyne Artistic Achievement Award for English Poetry at New York City College, where he earned his bachelor's degree (summa cum laude) in English, Journalism and African-American Studies. Okoampa-Ahoofe is the author of *Paa: A Tribute*, *Mmaa: I Miss You*, *Obaasima: Ideal Woman*, *Sororoscopes: Revised And Expanded*, *Ama Sefa: Unrequited Love*, *Dorkordicky Ponkorhythms: Wheel of Fortune*, *Atumpan: Drum-Talk*, *Odo Ye 'Wu: Love Is Till Death*, and *Sounds of Sirens: Essays in African Politics & Culture*, all of which titles are published by *iUniverse.com*. He has also been featured in *Downtown*. His early poems were performed on Ghana's national radio and television, as well as in the country's major cultural centers. He has also read and discussed his poetry, here in the United States, on Columbia University's WKCR radio program "The African Show" (FM 89.9)—hosted by Dr. Lawrence Nii Nartey. Okoampa-Ahoofe teaches English and Journalism at Nassau Community College of the State University of New York, Garden City. He has also taught Global African History at Mercy College, Dobbs Ferry, New York, and also at Indiana State University, Terre Haute. A graduate with master's and doctor of philosophy degrees from Temple University, Philadelphia, Okoampa-Ahoofe writes weekly political and cultural columns, as well as occasional book reviews, for the *New York Beacon*. He is married and has a daughter.

Praise For Okoampa-Ahoofe's Work

"Kwame Okoampa-Ahoofe's incisive analyses always expand the frontiers of our knowledge. He challenges what is taken for granted and in the process pushes us to reflect critically on important issues of the day. In his latest work, *The New Scapegoats*, Okoampa-Ahoofe re-visits old assumptions about the Africana world and takes to task how these assumptions are being re-cycled as the new paradigm for understanding Africa."—Karl Botchway, political scientist, New York City College of Technology, and author of *Understanding 'Development' Intervention in Northern Ghana*.

978-0-595-35011-7
0-595-35011-9